AMERICAN MAH JONGG PRIMER VOL 2

Essential Skills and Powerful Strategies
You Need to Optimize Your Winning Potential

MICHELE FRIZZELL

Paperback: April 2024

First e-book edition April 2024

Edited by David Frizzell

Cover art by Michele Frizzell

Illustrations by Michele Frizzell; icons and graphics courtesy of Canva Pro.

Printed by Amazon Kindle in the USA

Dedication

To my dad, who has always been my inspiration

for commitment, tenacity, and resilience.

Notes ...

Acknowledgments

> ## APPRECIATION
> ### IS A WONDERFUL THING
>
> IT MAKES WHAT IS EXCELLENT IN OTHERS
> BELONG TO US AS WELL

Voltaire, philosopher

Notes ...

Acknowledgments

When I first launched my YouTube channel, I thought nobody would find me, but I published videos anyway. I would not be where I am today without viewers.

Thank you for watching my videos and for joining me at livestreams. Your loyalty and support mean more to me than words can say.

Writing is not my forte. I suffer from writer's block on occasion, but once I get content out of my head onto a page, I find my groove. Then comes the final touch—editing. I would not be able to publish with confidence without other eyes on my work, so I want to thank my Angel Editors. Thank you for your constructive feedback and valuable suggestions.

To dig deep into any subject, one must research. Countless times, my research has taken me to Tom Sloper's website, Sloperama.com. Thank you for gifting the world with your genius.

Notes ...

Contents

Preface

> ## CHALLENGE IS CERTAIN
> ## DEFEAT IS A CHOICE

Roger Crawford, Hall of Fame Athlete

Preface

Why do humans like to play games? We are by nature curious and social creatures, so we seek to entertain ourselves and enjoy the company of friends. We also derive great value from the satisfaction that comes with challenging our minds.

Studies have shown that playing games offers many benefits. Most games rely on some degree of luck and vary in complexity. They are all designed to stimulate the imagination and contribute to the psychological, intellectual, and social development of the players[1].

Some games are so challenging that they qualify as mind sports. A mind sport is defined as any game of skill based on intellectual ability. Some games that rise to the level of being mind sports include chess, poker, and mah jongg[2]. You will see chess and poker briefly mentioned several times in this book, but we will focus on mah jongg, specifically American mah jongg.

American mah jongg is a tough game to learn, so I would venture to guess that you picked up this book because you want to build your skills and learn new strategies to make yourself a better player. Perhaps you have been surprised to hear about rules you were never taught, or maybe you have experienced a few losing streaks. You are clearly seeking to gain a deeper understanding of the game, and I applaud you for that.

---

[1] Dr. Jilas Paingeeri, 11/17/2022, Sprint Medical; Mental Health Benefits of Playing Card Games, https://tinyurl.com/2fdhvts3; Gamesver Team and JC Franco, 1/7/2024, 16 Ways Playing Card Games Can Help Your Mental Health, https://tinyurl.com/2fdhvts3.
Gamesver Team and JC Franco, 1/7/2024, 20 Powerful Benefits and Advantages of Playing Card Games. https://tinyurl.com/3yzyp9xv
[2] International Mind Sports Association, 2014/2002; https://imsa.sport/

Your knowledge of the game's rules allows you to play within the boundaries, while your ability to use skills like critical thinking, situational awareness, and social acuity can help you make smart decisions as you play the game. Your ability to choose the right strategies and apply tactics correctly can optimize your winning potential. The total package will equip you to play the game with greater confidence and, more times than not, give you a competitive edge.

In this book I will share everything I have learned about playing American mah jongg, including five epiphanies that have transformed the way I play and teach the game. The outcome is up to you. If you do the work, I have no doubt that you will find the game even more meaningful and rewarding.

Notes ...

Introduction

> **"** YOU CAN FIND MAGIC
> WHEREVER YOU LOOK.
> SIT BACK AND RELAX,
> ALL YOU NEED IS A BOOK. **"**

Dr. Seuss, author

Notes ...

Introduction

When I was 12 years old, my mother learned how to play Wright-Patterson mah jongg, and she taught me how to play so that she could practice at home. We did not realize it at the time, but we bonded over the tiles, and the game became our shared passion.

My sisters were too young to learn and my brothers were not interested in mah jongg, so they instead opted to play poker. If I wanted to belong, I had to join them. I learned the hand rankings, how to bet, and how to assess the potential of my hand; we were too young to calculate probabilities but had a great time, nonetheless. We travelled from household to household as we tested the limits of what our parents would allow regarding wins, losses, and disagreements. I continued to play poker on and off later in life and enjoyed it, but I always came back to mah jongg.

In poker, players can choose to participate in betting on outcomes based on their hand, community cards, and cards hidden in both opponents' hands and the deck. The player's position at the table determines when they can act, which can give them a strategic advantage. Asian versions of mah jongg share similarities with poker regarding position (e.g., wind of the round), tile efficiency (e.g., number tiles 4, 5, and 6), and whether to fold or play to win based on both hand value and the probability of being the first player to complete a hand. American mah jongg also contains these elements.

Over the years of playing mah jongg and running groups, I have had the pleasure of meeting people who have taught me other versions of the game. I have tested tactics, spent countless hours practicing, and studied lessons I learned from playing poker and Asian mah jongg variants. And I have had some epiphanies! These insights have enabled me to adapt concepts and modify strategies and tactics so that they can be applied to American mah jongg, raising the sophistication of the game and giving players an advantage at the table.

Merely reading this book will not guarantee that your win rate will increase. I can promise, however, that you will appreciate the game at a deeper level, and that you will enjoy playing more than ever before if you study the rules, practice newly adopted skills, apply tactics correctly, and keep a healthy mindset.

I know the journey will be challenging, and I'm ready to help you every step of the way, both in this book and online through the Mahj Life website[3].

---

[3] Mahj Life, https://mahjlife.com

How to Read this Book

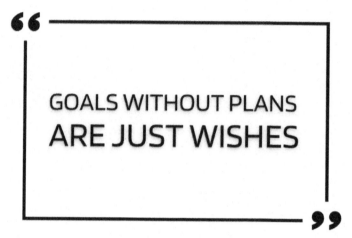

> ## GOALS WITHOUT PLANS
> ## ARE JUST WISHES

Antoine de Saint-Exupéry, author

Notes ...

How to Read this Book

Everyone learns differently. Bottom-up learners tend to absorb things best through a progressive approach made up of small sequential steps that build upon each other, ending with a complete concept. Top-down learners tend to prefer starting with the end in mind. They like to know what the result should look like and then take the steps needed to get there. Regardless of your learning style and your experience level, this book aims to deliver value.

If you find it helpful, most of the mah jongg terms used in this book can be found in a glossary on my website (Appendix A).

This book includes images of example hands for visual learners. To make this book timeless, I will be using a mock American mah jongg card. You can cut out a hard copy (Appendix D) or you can download and use a digital version[4]. As a reminder, "MAMJ" will precede the category and hand number. The following indicators will be used with the hands:

- Yellow lines will be used above the hands to show exposures.
- Yellow bars will be used to identify multiples (e.g., pair, pung, kong).
- Yellow boxes will be used to identify useful tiles, or keepers.
- Red boxes and bars will be used to identify discards.

I will use approximate numbers when referring to how many tiles remain in the wall for picking. These numbers will be preceded by the symbol ~ for approximately.

Please do not take the footnotes and appendices for granted, because they include resources for referenced content and continued learning in case you want to dive deeper into a topic.

---

[4] Mock American Mah Jongg digital card https://tinyurl.com/yfa3wcpm

New and Intermediate Players

You may have just finished taking lessons and want to shorten your learning curve. Welcome to the fast track! Buckle up because you're in for an exciting ride. Some of the topics in this book are advanced, which will be indicated by the bullseye icon below. Consider flagging those pages with a sticky note for a second read-through.

Or perhaps you have been playing for a while and you want to build your skills and learn new strategies. Welcome to the madness! After you integrate what you learn here into your playing style, you're going to knock the socks off your opponents!

Experienced Players

You may feel inclined to skip the more foundational content in this book. However, because my playing style is unconventional, I highly recommend that you read this book in its entirety. To explore advanced topics, look for this bullseye icon.

Welcome to the Growth Zone

Since you bought this book, I suspect you want to build your skills to gain confidence and learn new strategies to improve your performance and optimize your winning potential. If so, you will need to step out of your comfort zone and into the growth zone. If you are determined to grow, you need a plan!

The following is a five-step plan to ensure successful integration of new skills, strategies, and tactics:

Step 1: Use active learning strategies

Active learning strategies require you to engage in hands-on activities. We will cover some examples in chapter 2, "Essential Skills."

Using a study guide is another active learning strategy that can help you incorporate new concepts that pique your interest into your game. Consider purchasing the American Mah Jongg Primer Vol. 2 Companion Workbook for a turnkey solution.

Step 2: Play on different game platforms

There are several online platforms where you can play American mah jongg. I recommend Mahjong Time and I Love Mahj because each has its own strengths.

- I Love Mahj has a fantastic exercise room and robots with three levels of intelligence.
- Mahjong Time has the most realistic look and feel to the game so you can practice surveying discards and hand reading.

If you have not tried either of these, you can sign up for an extended trial through my affiliate partnership to practice your new skills and strategies (Appendix F).

Step 3: Set clear goals

Setting clear goals is key to measuring your progress. Consider using one of several mnemonic devices that has been proven to optimize goal setting (e.g., SMART, SMARTER, PACT). The American Mah Jongg Primer Vol. 2 Companion Workbook uses PACT—Purposeful, Actionable, Continuous, and Trackable. I prefer this mnemonic because it's concise but powerful.

Step 4: Consider working with a mentor

American mah jongg is gaining in popularity, and many avid players have become instructors to share their passion with others. I highly recommend finding an instructor. If you cannot find one in your area, you can search for one online. The Mahj Life Instructor Guild has members ready to serve you. As guild members, instructors have access to all game rules and have learned teaching methodologies to ensure they deliver value to their students. Visit the Mahj Life instructor directory to find a mentor to help you integrate what you learn into your playing style (Appendix C).

Step 5: Practice whenever you can

Practice makes progress, so practice online and in person. Also, pull out your tiles and use hands-on drills to test the new skills and tactics you will learn in this book. In Chapter 2, the Charleston Modeling section offers several hands-on skill building exercises.

Are you ready? Let's get started by looking at the rules of American mah jongg so that we can build a firm foundation.

CHAPTER ONE
Know the Rules

> THE CAPACITY TO LEARN IS A GIFT.
> THE ABILITY TO LEARN IS A SKILL.
> THE WILLINGNESS TO LEARN IS A CHOICE.

Brian Herbert, author

Notes ...

Chapter 1: Know the Rules

Nuances of American Mah Jongg

The National Mah Jongg League (the League) was established by a group of New York City players in 1937. They found that Americans were confused about the many ways to play mah jongg, so they created their own rules for social games. The following five features of the American game differentiate it from other versions of mah jongg:

1. The Annual Card

The League developed an annual player reference card (the card) listing the winning pattern-based combinations, or hands. The objective in American mah jongg is to be the first player to complete one of the hands on the card with their tiles.

The hands are organized into categories based on the shape of a hand and/or the type of tiles used. Hands are described using colors, letters, and numbers, followed by text in parentheses that explains any flexibility or limitations for a given hand. Also, each hand is marked as either exposable (X) or concealed (C) and has a value relating to its level of difficulty to complete (Fig. 1.1).

YEAR		VALUE	QUINTS		VALUE	WINDS - DRAGONS		VALUE
FF YYYY DDDD DDDD (Any 1 suit with any 2 Dragons)	X	25	11 222 3333 44444 (Any 4 consecutive #s)	X	40	NNNN EEEE WWWWW SS	X	25
YYYY NNNN RR 5555 (Red Dragon only)	X	25	1111 11111 DDDD (Any 3 suits, any like numbers)	X	40	FF NNNN RRRR 5555 (Red Dragon only)	X	25
YYYY EEEE GG WWWW (Green Dragon only)	X	25	FF NNNNN DD 5555 (Red Dragon only)	X	45	FF EEEE GGGG WWWWW (Green Dragon only)	X	25
FS YYYY DDDD NEWS (Any 2 suits)	C	30	FF WWWWW DD WWWWW (Green Dragon only)	X	45	NNNN 11 11 11 5555 (Any 3 suits, any like odd #s)	X	30
						EEEE 22 22 22 WWWW (Any 3 suits, any like even #s)	X	30
2468			**CONSECUTIVE RUN**			DDDD DD DDDD NEWS (Dragons any combination)	C	30
2222 4444 6666 88 (Any 1 suit)	X	25	11 222 3333 444 55 or 55 666 7777 888 99 (Any 1 suit)	X	25			
22 44 666 888 DDDD (Any 3 suits)	X	25	111 2222 333 4444 55 (Any 2 suits, any 4 con #s)	X	25	**369**		
FFFF 22 44 666 888 (Any 1 suit)	X	25	FF 111 222 333 444 (Any 2 suits, any 4 con #s)	X	25	3333 6666 9999 DD (Any 1 suit)	X	25
FF 22 44 6666 8888 (Any 3 suits)	X	30	FFFF 1111 2222 DD or FFFF 1111 2222 DD (Any 2 con #s)	X	25	FF 333 666 999 DDD (Any 2 suits)	X	25
FF 222 44 66 888 DD (Any 2 suits)	X	30	FF 11 22 333 444 DD (Any 3 suits, any 4 con #s)	X	30	FFFF 3333 66 9999 or FFFF 3333 66 9999	X	25
222 44 66 888 NEWS (Any 1 suit)	C	30	11 22 33 4444 5555 (Any 3 suits, any 5 con #s)	X	30	FF 3333 6666 9999 or FF 3333 6666 9999	X	25
			1111 22 3333 NEWS (Any 1 suit, any 3 con #s)	C	30	33 66 99 3333 3333 (Any 3 suits, kongs can be 3, 6, or 9)	X	30
LIKE NUMBERS						FF 333 66 999 NEWS (Any 1 suit)	C	30
FF 1111 1111 1111 (Any 3 suits, any like #s)	X	25	**13579**					
FF 1111 1111 NEWS (Any 2 suits, any like #s)	C	30	11 333 5555 777 99 (Any 1 suit)	X	25	**SINGLES AND PAIRS**		
			111 3333 333 5555 or 555 7777 777 9999 (Any 2 suits)	X	25	NN EE WW SS 11 11 11 (Any like numbers)	C	50
ADDITION			FF 1111 3333 5555 or FF 5555 7777 9999 (Any 1 suit)	X	25	FF 22 44 66 88 DD DD (Any 3 suits)	C	50
FFFF 2222 + 8888 = 10 or FFFF 2222 + 8888 = 10	X	25	111 333 555 777 99 (Any 3 suits)	X	25	FF 11 33 55 77 99 DD (Any 1 suit)	C	50
FFFF 3333 + 7777 = 10 or FFFF 3333 + 7777 = 10	X	25	FF 111 333 555 DDD or FF 555 777 999 DDD (Any 2 suits)	X	25	11 22 33 44 55 66 77 (Any one suit, any 7 con #s)	C	50
FFFF 6666 + 4444 = 10 or FFFF 6666 + 4444 = 10	X	25	FFFF 11 33 55 DDDD or FFFF 55 77 99 DDDD (Any 1 suit)	X	30	33 66 99 33 66 99 DD (Any 3 suits)	C	50
FFFF 9999 + 1111 = 10 or FFFF 9999 + 1111 = 10	X	25	1111 33 5555 NEWS or 5555 77 9999 NEWS (Any 1 suit)	C	30	FF YYYY YYYY NEWS (Any 2 suits)	C	75

Figure 1.1 Mahj Life mock American mah jongg card (MAMJ)

It is important to note that the colors on the card do not dictate which suits should be used. A change in color on the card simply indicates a change of suit in the hand. The player decides which color on the card represents each suit in the hand unless the League includes text in parentheses next to that hand indicating otherwise.

For a deep dive into the card for the current year, watch my video and check out my free card analysis eBook (Appendix B).

2. Flowers

There are eight flowers in a mah jongg set. In American mah jongg, the flowers are not bonus tiles, as they are in most other versions of the game, but components of nearly half of the hands on the card.

3. Jokers

There are eight jokers in an American mah jongg set. Jokers are wild cards, and a player can use any number of them in blocks of three or more identical tiles, such as a pung (three of a kind), kong (four of a kind), or quint (five of a kind) – I call these "multiples." To be clear, a joker cannot be used as a tile in a block of single tiles, such as blocks for the year or NEWS; or as a tile in a pair (a block of two identical tiles).

The presence of jokers in the American game often leads to a misconception that this version involves more luck than other versions of the game. However, jokers are necessary logistically because the card has a limited number of hands to choose from, and all hands require various combinations of multiples.

4. Multiples

A standard mah jongg hand typically consists of four blocks of three or four tiles (e.g., chow [three tiles in a sequence; prominent in Chinese versions], pung, kong) plus a pair. In American mah jongg, there are no exposable chows (block of three single consecutive numbers, such as 123). American mah jongg hands consist of various combinations of single tiles, pairs, pungs, kongs, and quints.

5. The Charleston

A hand of American mah jongg has three phases:

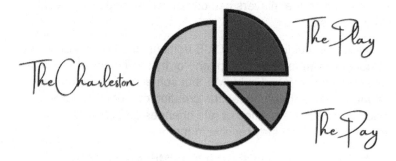

Figure 1.3 Phases of a Game

The Charleston is a "hand development accelerator" because this is when players have opportunities to transform their hand with up to 21 tiles in up to seven passes. The number of tiles passed between players nearly equates to a full wall!

This process is not exclusive to American mah jongg using National Mah Jongg League rules. It's also used in Wright Patterson Mah Jongg and Western Mahjong. I have even seen a video of people playing a Taiwanese game with a variation of the Charleston where they passed three tiles to the left, three times!

The Play begins after the Charleston when East discards their 14th tile and players pick and discard one tile at a time to continue hand development.

The Pay concludes a game if someone declares mah jongg. The other players pay the winner the value of their hand.

Where to Find the Rules

American mah jongg requires critical thinking, situational awareness, and social acuity. Because of these complexities, a detailed set of rules exists to prevent chaos and conflict.

Mah Jongg Made Easy (MJME) is the official guidebook the League publishes to ensure fairness when playing relaxed games in social settings. Therefore, these guidelines often use words like "should" rather than words like "must." If you use social media, you will also discover different house rules some groups use so that players can customize gameplay based on their interests.

Between the publication of MJME editions, the League answers questions from members by phone or by snail mail. Often these answers can be found in MJME, but sometimes an unforeseen situation arises that requires the creation of a new guideline or rule. Members are notified of rule changes and clarifications in the annual bulletin they receive in the mail.

A challenge all players face is that MJME is not published digitally, and the League does not post rule changes and clarifications consistently on its website. Therefore, many members remain unaware of these changes. To fill this gap, Mahj Life maintains a mah jongg wiki, a free, searchable, on-demand collection of mah jongg-centric articles that includes guidelines, rules, strategies, game etiquette, teaching tips, and more[5]. Each article cites guidelines and rules issued by the League. The articles are categorized by subject matter and are labeled with keyword tags shown in the article footer to allow online navigation.

---

[5] Mahj Life Wiki; https://mahjlife.com/wiki

Here is a list of Mahj Life wiki articles containing guidelines and rules that players should review frequently:

- Rules not in MJME (article 00)
- Top 10 Confusing and Complex Rules (article 189)
- Rules without Penalties (article 195)
- Reasons for Disqualification (article 24)
- Playing with a Pie (article 145)
- Common House Rules (article 50)

After you have studied the guidelines and rules, I invite you to test your knowledge. Join my mailing list and select "mah jongg quizzes."[6] I will send you an email with instructions.

Game rules set boundaries to ensure fair play. The next step is for you to figure out how best to play within those boundaries by developing skills that can optimize your winning potential.

---

[6] Mahj Life Email List; https://mahjlife.com/email-list-subscription

Notes ...

CHAPTER TWO
Acquire Essential Skills

Notes ...

Chapter 2: Acquire Essential Skills

Game Theory

Game theory (Epiphany #1) is "a theoretical framework for conceiving social situations among competing players"[7]. In other words, it is the study and application of strategic decision-making based on information gathered by observing how people act and interact when playing a game. The mah jongg showdown between the main characters in the movie Crazy Rich Asians is an excellent example. Have no fear, though. We are only peeking inside of this rabbit hole.

Using game theory to your advantage means learning how to make decisions based on everything you know at any given moment. In addition to your own internal thought process, you will need to consider external variables that can affect gameplay dynamics, such as:

- Setting
  - In-person
  - Online
- Format
  - Social
  - Competitive
- Players
  - Experience level
  - Knowledge of rules
  - Strategy application
  - Style of play

When gathering intel by observing your opponents, you need to also keep in mind that, while humans are creatures of habit, they can also be unpredictable.

---

[7] Karpel, Katie Kerpel. 2023. "*Game Theory,*" Investopedia
https://www.investopedia.com/terms/g/gametheory.asp

You can develop the following three skills to use game theory to your advantage in American mah jongg: critical thinking, situational awareness, and social acuity.

Essential Skills

Critical Thinking

Critical thinking is "self-guided, self-disciplined thinking which attempts to reason at the highest level of quality in a fair-minded way."[8] Practical application of critical thinking helps us with the disciplined process of assessing and integrating information gathered from observation, experience, reflection, reasoning, and communication. Critical thinking comes naturally for some people, but, for others, it requires practice.

To illuminate how critical thinking applies to playing mah jongg, here are examples of how you can use it during the Charleston:

- Observe—Remember which kinds of tiles are being passed (or not passed) to help you optimize your hand development.

- Interpret—Realize that when a player passes blind, they are either between hands and unable to decide, or they have a well-developed hand without three unwanted tiles to pass.

- Decide—Evaluate the development of your hand after the first left; if you have three tiles to pass, continue with the second Charleston. Otherwise, stop the Charleston.

- Execute—Choose misfit tiles, such as tiles that do not fit into the category you are playing, to pass and mitigate risk by selecting the misfit tiles that will make your pass more defensive (covered in chapter 3, "Adopt Powerful Strategies," in "Hoptoi's Strategy by Wall").

This process is multifaceted and cyclical. You will need to continually observe your opponents' actions and interactions while focusing on your own hand development (covered in chapter 3, "Situational Awareness," and "Social Acuity").

---

[8] Paul, Richard and Elder, Linda. 2008. "*The Miniature Guide to Critical Thinking Concepts and Tools*," Foundation for Critical Thinking Press, 2008; https://www.criticalthinking.org/pages/our-conception-of-critical-thinking/411

Charleston Drills and the Mock Charleston

Think of the Charleston as a powerful pre-game hand development accelerator. The following hands-on Charleston drills will allow you to fine-tune your critical thinking skills and can also help you familiarize yourself with hands more quickly whenever the League publishes a new card.

To do these drills, you will need to stage a mock Charleston (Fig. 2.1.1-2.1.34). It's called a mock Charleston because it is not meant to be an exact representation. This process simulates the experience of receiving passed tiles from other players so that you can practice making decisions during this phase of the game. To see a video demonstration of staging a mock Charleston, see appendix B, "Direct Links to NMJL YouTube Videos."

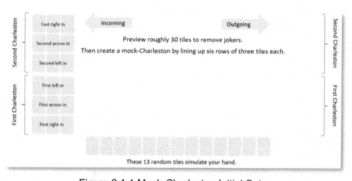

Figure 2.1.1 Mock-Charleston Initial Setup

Figure 2.1.2 Select first right out

Figure 2.1.3 First right out

Figure 2.1.4 Take first right

Figure 2.1.5 First right in

Figure 2.1.6 Select first across out

Figure 2.1.7 First across out

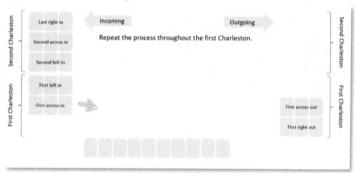

Figure 2.1.8 Take first across

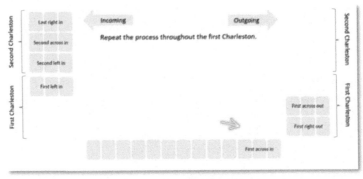

Figure 2.1.9 First across in

Figure 2.1.10 Select first left out

Figure 2.1.11 First left out

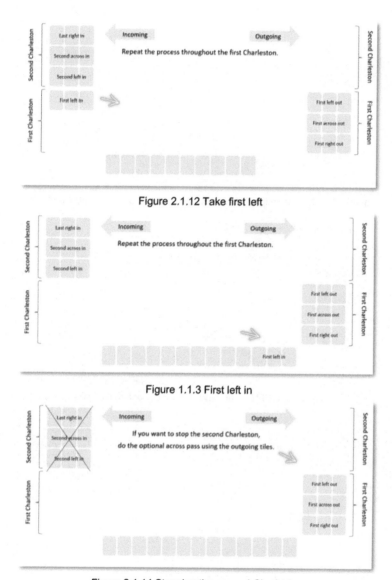

Figure 2.1.12 Take first left

Figure 1.1.3 First left in

Figure 2.1.14 Stopping the second Charleston

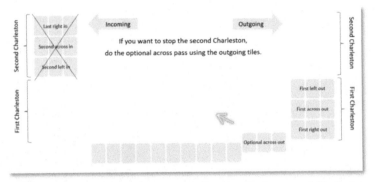

Figure 2.1.15 Select optional across out after stopping the second Charleston

Figure 2.1.16 Mix outgoing tiles for the optional across

Figure 2.1.17 Take optional across

Figure 2.1.18 Optional across in

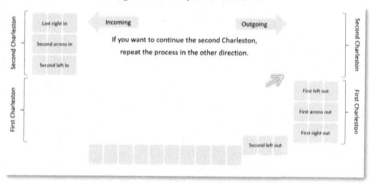

Figure 2.1.19 Continuing the Charleston, select second left out

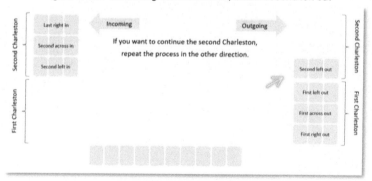

Figure 2.1.20 Second left out

Figure 2.1.21 Take second left

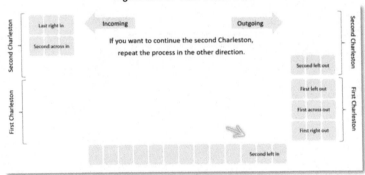

Figure 2.1.22 Second left in

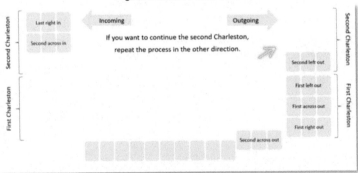

Figure 2.1.23 Select second across out

20

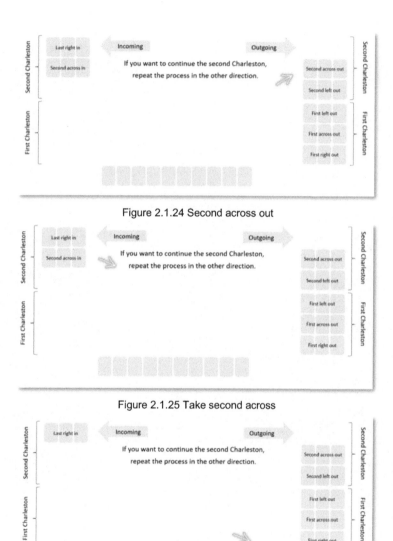

Figure 2.1.24 Second across out

Figure 2.1.25 Take second across

Figure 2.1.26 Second across in

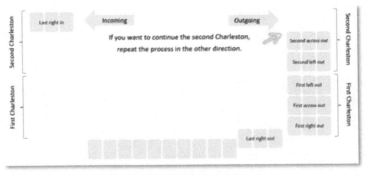

Figure 2.1.27 Select last right out

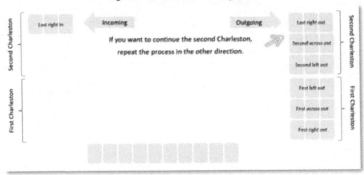

Figure 2.1.28 Last right out

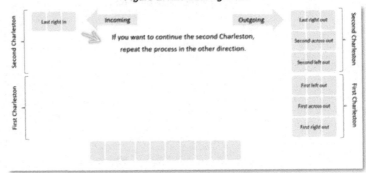

Figure 2.1.29 Take last right

Second Charleston

First Charleston

Outgoing

If you want to continue the second Charleston,
repeat the process in the other direction.

Last right out
Second across out
Second left out

First left out
First across out
First right out

Second Charleston

First Charleston

Last right in

Figure 2.1.30 Last right in

Second Charleston

First Charleston

Outgoing

The optional across is the final pass using the outgoing tiles.

Last right out
Second across out
Second left out

First left out
First across out
First right out

Second Charleston

First Charleston

Figure 2.1.31 Select optional across out

Second Charleston

First Charleston

Mix the outgoing tiles and take as many tiles as you
want to pass to complete the Charleston.

Second Charleston

First Charleston

Figure 2.1.32 Mix outgoing tiles for the optional across

Figure 2.1.33 Optional across out

Figure 2.1.34 Optional across in

Remember that you have the prerogative to pass fewer than three tiles on the first left and last right of the Charleston. Passing blind means that you can supplement your pass using tiles from the incoming pass to fulfill the obligation of passing three tiles. This option is called "passing blind" because you are not supposed to look at the supplemental tiles.

The following drills use the mock Charleston method above, but each serves a different purpose focused on a specific skill (Appendix B, "NMJL YouTube Videos"):

Charleston Modeling
The purpose of this exercise is to practice decision making during the Charleston. By doing this exercise, you will build confidence in your decision making and learn to appreciate the power of the Charleston.

1. Create a mock Charleston with no jokers.
2. Identify the strength of the hand and choose a category based on this strength and potential supporting tiles.
3. Proceed with the Charleston gathering tiles that support the strength of your hand.
4. Document your results (e.g., category, hand, number of discards left at the end of the mock Charleston) to track your progress.

Charleston Chain Reaction
This exercise tests your instincts. You will see that almost any category you choose can work with your tiles if you make the right decisions at the right time.

1. The setup for this exercise is the same as for Charleston Modeling, but this time grab your camera so that you can document your dealt hand and take a picture of each incoming pass.
2. Identify the strength of the hand and choose a category based on this strength and potential supporting tiles for Plan A and a different potential category for Plan B.
3. Proceed with the Charleston and make decisions that focus on Plan A. Document your results (e.g., category, hand, number of discards at the end of the Charleston) for comparison later.
4. Recreate your dealt hand and each of the incoming passes using the photos.
5. Replay the Charleston with these same incoming passes making decisions focused on Plan B.
6. Compare the results to see which plan worked better.

Charleston Force

The purpose of this exercise is to practice developing hands in preselected categories. This exercise is also good practice for competitive events because sometimes there are prizes for the first player to win a hand in a preselected category. This exercise will force you out of your comfort zone by encouraging you to play hands you might not normally consider.

1. The setup is the same as for Charleston Modeling, but this time you need to label one index card for each category on the card.
2. Mix up the index cards and then pick three random categories.
3. Go through the Charleston Modeling exercise three times and force yourself to make a hand in a different one of the preselected categories each time.

Charleston Sprints

The purpose of this exercise is to practice making top-speed decisions during a mock-Charleston in three iterations known as "sprints." This is a good skill to develop if you ever play games with time constraints. For example, playing online requires players to make decisions within 8-10 seconds and playing in tournaments requires players to complete four games in 55 minutes.

1. The setup is the same as for Charleston Modeling, but this time you need a stopwatch, or the stopwatch function on your smart phone, to time your decision making.
2. Complete five laps, each consisting of three sprints and the setups in between.
3. Remove the setup time from each lap and average the sprint times for the three sprints.

Use these time thresholds as a guide:
- For novice players, the average time should be under four minutes per sprint.
- For intermediate players, the average time should be under three minutes.
- For advanced players, the average time should be under two minutes.

These Charleston drills will help you develop critical thinking skills related to mah jongg so that you can enjoy the game even more, both in person and when playing online.

Situational Awareness

Skill-based games are designed with pathways to victory allowing players to apply different strategies throughout the game. Just like a good story, these games have a beginning, a middle, and an end. In mah jongg, the pathways of the game are determined by the wall in play and the stages are called the begin-game, the middle-game, and the end-game.

Situational awareness, as it applies to mah jongg, involves being cognizant of what stage the game is in and noticing what is happening at the table. This awareness will allow you to better understand how information, your opponents' actions, and your own actions will affect the game's outcome.

There are three main components of situational awareness:

1. Perception: Recognize sources of information available (e.g., discards, exposures).
2. Comprehension: Interpret information gathered so that you can use it to make the right decisions at the right time (e.g., identify categories being played by using a process of elimination).
3. Anticipation: Predict how the game will progress and adapt to changes (e.g., estimate potential to win based on your number of discards compared to the number of tiles left for picking).

Using situational awareness will allow you to recognize risks and assess potential rewards so that you can perceive and effectively respond to situations as they unfold. Situational awareness requires keenly observing your opponent's actions (e.g., discards and exposures) to gather information. As you observe your opponents, analyze the information so that you can make good decisions as you focus on developing your hand.

The following are examples of how you can use situational awareness to your advantage when playing mah jongg.

Figure 2.2.1 The Charleston

During the Charleston (Fig. 2.2.1):

- Remember the types of tiles your opponent's pass.
- Remember who passes blind.
- Watch for tiles that are passed repeatedly.
- Notice which tiles are not passed.
- Remember who, if anyone, stops the Charleston.
- Remember the number of tiles passed in the optional across.

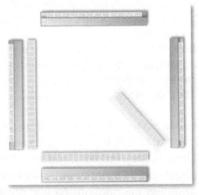

Figure 2.2.2 Begin-Game

Begin-Game, 99 tiles remaining (Fig. 2.2.2):

- Watch discards and use the process of elimination to identify likely categories being played.

- If any player calls a discard and makes an exposure this early in the game, they likely have a well-developed hand, or they are making an early commitment that could hinder them later.
- Each exposure reveals information about the hands being played.

Figure 2.2.3 Begin-Game

Middle-Game, Part 1, 80-60 tiles remaining (Fig. 2.2.3):

- Heighten your awareness of discards because they will become increasingly more meaningful.

Middle-Game, Part 2, 60-41 tiles remaining:

- Discards right after an exposure become increasingly more meaningful.
- Monitor exposures and discards and use the process of elimination to confirm likely hands being played.

Figure 2.2.4 End-Game

End-Game, 40 tiles remaining (Fig. 2.2.4):

- A player rearranging tiles may indicate that player has decided to fold.
- A player making exposures in the end-game is likely playing to win. If a player has decided to fold, there is no good reason for that player to make an exposure. Doing so reveals information, and any jokers used become available to other players if the natural tiles are in their hands or in the wall.

Situational awareness skills are also used when reading your opponent's hands. By surveying discards, monitoring exposures, and observing your opponent's behaviors you can gather intel that can be used to help you make good decisions as you develop your hand, and it can even help you play defensively. Here are some examples:

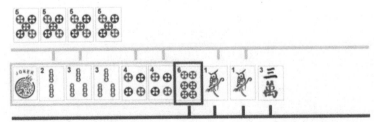

Figure 2.3.1 Reading hands in the begin-game; MAMJ Consecutive Run #2

Interpretation: A player claimed a discard to make a kong of 5 dots and they discarded a 6 dot. Opponents could predict that they are not playing Consecutive Run with big tiles.

Begin-Game, 90 tiles remaining:

- When a player makes an exposure in the begin-game, there are three probable reasons (Fig. 2.3.1):
    1. They have the tiles and want to seize the opportunity for a pure exposure.
    2. They are new to the game and have not learned about hand development and timing.
    3. They are experienced and have decided to expedite hand development for a strong hand.
- Watch their discards to eliminate the categories on which they are not focused.

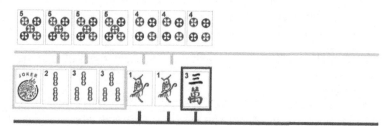

Figure 2.3.2 Reading hands in the middle-game; MAMJ Consecutive Run #2

Interpretation: The second exposure was a 4 dot pung, and they discarded a 3 crak so they are likely playing with 2-3 bams.

Middle-Game, 60 tiles remaining (Fig. 2.3.2):

- When a player makes an exposure in the middle-game, they likely know what hand they are playing.
- Make note of the tile they discard just after their exposures as the game progresses to confirm the category they are likely playing.
- Survey the other discards in front of them to confirm the category they are focused on; also consider any previous exposures.

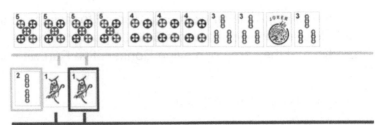

Figure 2.3.3 Reading hands in the end-game; MAMJ Consecutive Run #2

Interpretation: The third exposure was a 3 bam with a joker up for grabs so they are likely close to ready.

End-Game, 40 tiles remaining (Fig. 2.3.3):

- When a player makes an exposure in the end-game, they are likely playing to win.
- Consider your potential to win based on your number of discards, number of picks left in the wall, and the number of your tiles that are visible in discards or exposures.

We will go into greater detail with each of these examples in the next chapter.

If you want to watch video demonstrations of how to develop your skills online, the Mahj Life wiki has an article titled "American Mah Jongg Skills and Strategies Matrix (article 210)" that includes a schedule of recurring topics with links to the latest videos and related articles (Appendix B).

Social Acuity

Social acuity in mah jongg is the ability to read cues from players at the table. Since mah jongg is a social game, social acuity can provide you with an advantage as you observe your opponents' actions and interactions. Their behaviors, or "tells," contain clues that, when interpreted correctly, can provide insight into their situations, and help you make better decisions during a game.

As you observe your opponents, consider that their actions may be based on their perceived position in the game based on the strength of the hand, number of discards in the hand, number of discards visible, and number of picks left in the wall:

Underdog: The back or weak perceived position

Contender: Middle or moderate perceived position

Frontrunner: Front or strong perceived position

Keep in mind that players can bluff, meaning that they may try to deceive you by acting in a way contrary to their intentions and position:

> Someone in an underdog position may make an exposure in the end-game to mislead their opponents into thinking they are still in the game when, in fact, they know they cannot win.

> Someone in a contender position may not call a needed tile to make an exposure with a joker to mitigate the risk of an exchange in the begin-game.

> Someone in a frontrunner position is waiting for a single tile to complete a pair. They may discard a natural tile from a larger block, such as a pung or a kong, if they have enough jokers to complete the hand without that tile. That way, the player doesn't have to discard a joker, which often persuades opponents into folding and playing more defensively to block the player, who appears to be in an extremely strong position, from winning.

You should assess your position throughout the game to manage your expectations and determine appropriate levels of risk you take as you develop your hand. We'll talk more about this in Hoptoi's Strategy by Wall.

Noticing your opponents' tells is another way to gain an advantage. In mah jongg, there are three types of tells (Fig. 2.4.1-2.4.10):

Verbal Tells

Verbal tells are spoken words that give away information about a player's hand. If you listen attentively to conversation during the game, you can gather useful information. I remember playing with someone who said that her favorite hands are the ones with dragons. Can you guess which tiles I did not pass to her during the Charleston? If you guessed that I did not pass her dragons, you guessed right!

Figure 2.4.1 Verbal Tell, I got nothin!

Interpretation: After tiles have been distributed, a player complains about not knowing what to do with their tiles (Fig. 2.4.1).

Figure 2.4.2 Verbal Tell, I went the wrong way.

Interpretation: During the Charleston, a player says that they chose the wrong category to play (Fig. 2.4.2).

Figure 2.4.3 Verbal Tell, I can't buy a flower!

Interpretation: During the middle-game, a player shares that they can't get flowers (Fig. 2.4.3).

Figure 2.4.4 Verbal Tell, where are the jokers?!

Interpretation: During the end-game, a player laments about not having jokers (Fig. 2.4.4).

Physical Tells

Physical tells are micro expressions and body language reactions. Opponents often exhibit physical tells after a discard or exposure.

Figure 2.4.5 Physical Tell, Hesitation

Interpretation: During the middle-game, a tile is discarded and a player hesitates before picking a tile from the wall indicating that they are likely in between categories or hands (Fig. 2.4.5).

Figure 2.4.6 Physical Tell, Flinch

Interpretation: During the middle-game, a tile is discarded and a player flinches indicating that they needed it but could not take it (Fig. 2.4.6).

Tile Tells

Tile tells are how players arrange, move, and manipulate the tiles in their hand.

Figure 2.4.7 Spaces

Interpretation: This player may have a pair, five keepers, and six discards or Plan B.
Spaces between groups of tiles on a rack tell you that a player is a beginner and may be separating out discards or organizing tiles by meld. An experienced player would not give away this kind of information (Fig. 2.4.7).

Figure 2.4.8 Tile Tell, Tilts

Interpretation: Tile manipulation may be showing where needed tiles have been discarded. A tilted tile often indicates that a tile that the player needs has been discarded. Some players tilt tiles this way to help them keep track of the status of needed tiles (Fig. 2.4.8).

Figure 2.4.9 Tile Tell, Placement

Interpretation: After several games, it was observed that this player placed jokers to their left so when they pick a tile and place it to their left, it is likely a joker which can be confirmed by physical tells like a Cheshire cat smile. Players often place jokers near one end of their rack. If a new tile is placed at the end of the rack, it might be a joker (Fig. 2.4.9).

Figure 2.4.10 Tile Tell, placement

Interpretation: After several games, it was observed that this player placed flowers to their right so when they pick a tile and place it to their right, it is likely a flower which can be confirmed by physical tells like a raise of the eyebrows. Players often place flowers similarly to how they place jokers. If a new tile is placed near one end of the rack, it might be a flower (Fig. 2.4.10).

With practice, you can learn to use social acuity skills to improve your play. Pay close attention to what is happening at the table— listen to what is being said and watch for micro expressions and body language. Observe your opponents and interpret their tells to make educated guesses about possible categories or hands they might be playing and how their hands are developing. Tells can help you make decisions about which strategies to use to thwart your opponents' hands development or to further your own hand development.

Remember that your opponents can also use social acuity, so it is crucial to exercise self-awareness and self-regulation. Monitor your thoughts, emotions, language, behaviors, and reactions when playing the game to minimize your own tells.

Using Poker Psychology and Strategies in American Mah Jongg

Social scientists and game enthusiasts have been studying poker psychology since the late 1970s, and many of the concepts they describe can be adapted and applied to mah jongg. Profiling players (Epiphany #2) is one of these concepts. The purpose of profiling players is to identify an opponent's playing style, which can reveal useful information. Each playing style has characteristics and tendencies that can help you predict how a game may progress.

Mah jongg, like poker, is a game of observation. Fully reading the table requires reading hands and identifying playing styles. If you pay attention, you can gather information that should provide a competitive and strategic advantage at the table.

The better you know your opponents, the easier it will be to identify their playing styles and decide whether you need to adjust your tactics to counter theirs. Remember that humans are creatures of habit, but we can also be clever and unpredictable. There are two important variables to consider when profiling players:

1. A player's personality makes them unique, and their playing style may change as they build their skills and learn new strategies.
2. A player might also adjust their playing style based on:
   - Their opponents
     - Level of experience: beginner, intermediate, advanced
     - Style of play: passive, assertive
   - The strength of their hand
     - Gaps: one or more missing components in their hand (e.g., missing a pair of Norths)
     - Weaknesses: one or more "shallow" components, an inadequate quantity of a tile for a big multiple (e.g., singles that need to be pairs, pairs that need to be a bigger multiple)
     - Vulnerability: the tiles needed have been discarded or are in exposures

- The format of the game
  - Social: casual atmosphere and lenient with rules
  - Competitive: formal atmosphere and strict with rules

Playing Styles

Two main factors determine playing styles in American mah jongg: flexibility and risk tolerance. In American mah jongg, potential winning hands are limited to those listed on the card, and it is tempting to try to pick a hand immediately from your dealt tiles. Doing this is called playing with a fixed approach. You could play this way, and it would not be wrong, but don't be surprised if you get stuck with a hand that is unviable later in the game. To play more flexibly, you can instead choose a category to focus on based on the strength in your dealt hand and then gather tiles that can be used for any hand in that category. Picking a hand is deferred until you are left with only tiles that can be used in that category. This method uses an adaptive approach because you are giving yourself the freedom and flexibility to adapt what hand you are playing based on what happens as the game progresses. We will cover the fixed and adaptive approaches in the next chapter as they apply to hand development.

At the same time, American mah jongg is a tile-melding game where players can expedite hand development by claiming discards to make an exposure. Some players hesitate to make an exposure, especially if that exposure uses jokers, because they can lose these jokers in an exchange to another player with the natural tile. Some players, on the other hand, are quick to claim a discard for an exposure with jokers despite knowing the risk of losing them.

These factors distinguish players on the flexibility and risk tolerance spectrums (Fig. 2.5.1):

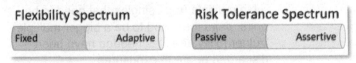

Figure 2.5.1 Playing style spectrums

On these spectrums, there is no right or wrong; there is simply a difference. Players can have tendencies anywhere in both spectrums. This graph shows one spectrum on each axis and separates playing styles into quadrants (Fig. 2.5.2):

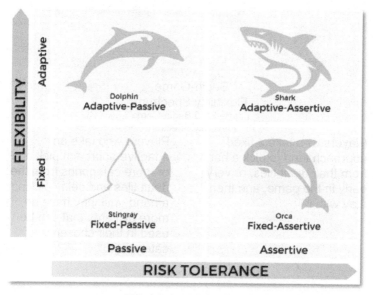

Figure 2.5.2 Playing style chart

As players develop skills and adopt new strategies, they might move from one quadrant to another. They may also move from one quadrant to another depending on the game setting.

Following are examples of what you might observe when playing the game:

Begin-Game
Flexibility Spectrum
Figure 2.5.3 Begin-Game
Flexibility Spectrum

Players who take a fixed approach tend to pick a hand from their dealt tiles, or very early in the game, and then stay with it.

Players who take an adaptive approach pick one or more categories from the dealt tiles and delay picking a hand until they have no more discards that can be used in their chosen categories.

Middle-Game
Risk Tolerance
Spectrum
Figure 2.5.4 Middle-Game
Risk Tolerance Spectrum

Passive players tend to delay their first exposure to control information, especially if that exposure requires using a joker.

Assertive players tend to claim discards and make exposures to expedite hand development regardless of risk.

End-Game
Risk Tolerance
Spectrum

Figure 2.5.5 End-Game Risk
Tolerance Spectrum

Passive players tend to fold and break up their hand to discard safely earlier than other players.

Assertive players tend to play to win regardless of risk.

Study the following playing style profiles so that you will know what to look for as you get to know your opponents.

Stingray
Fixed-Passive

General Characteristics
- Risk-averse
- Noncompetitive
- Plays in a state of uncertainty

Likely Tactics
- Limits hands
- Picks a hand before the Charleston and stays with it
- Waits to claim a discard to make their first exposure until they know what hand they are playing
- Makes exposures with jokers if there is minimal exchange potential
- Switches to defense earlier than other players

Advantages
- Simplified decision making due to a narrow focus

Disadvantages
- Misses out on needed tiles
- Limited switchability due to missed opportunities to call discards
- Least likely to win

Defensive Maneuvers
- Play assertively

Dolphin
Adaptive-Passive

General Characteristics
- Risk-averse
- Noncompetitive
- Plays in a state of caution

Likely Tactics
- Picks a category based on the strength of their hand and does not pick a hand until they have all useful tiles
- Waits to claim a discard to make their first exposure until they know what hand they are playing
- Makes exposures with jokers if there is minimal exchange potential
- Switches to defense earlier than other players

Advantages
- Adaptability
- Flexibility

Disadvantages
- Misses out on needed tiles

Defensive Maneuvers
- Play assertively

Orca
Fixed-Assertive

General Characteristics
- Risk-tolerant
- Competitive
- Plays in a state of belief

Likely Tactics
- Limits hands
- Picks a hand before the Charleston and stays with it
- Claims discards early to expedite hand development
- Claims discards with jokers regardless of exchange potential
- Plays to win if ready in the end-game regardless of discarding risky tiles

Advantages
- Simplified decision making due to a narrow focus

Disadvantages
- May get stuck because of committing to a hand with early exposures
- Limited switchability due to missed opportunities to call discards

Defensive Maneuvers
- Use hand reading to figure out what they are playing and adjust your game plan
- Sabotage their hand during the middle-game
- Fold early and block the player from winning
- Watch for disqualification opportunities

Shark
Adaptive-Assertive

General Characteristics
- Risk-tolerant
- Competitive
- Plays in a state of confidence

Likely Tactics
- Picks a category based on the strength of their hand and does not pick a hand until they have all useful tiles
- Claims discards early if they know what hand they are playing
- Claims discards with jokers regardless of exchange potential
- Plays to win if ready in the end-game regardless of discarding risky tiles

Advantages
- Adaptability
- Flexibility

Disadvantages
- May get stuck because of committing to a hand with early exposures.

Defensive Maneuvers
- Use hand reading to figure out what they are playing and adjust your game plan
- Sabotage their hand during the middle-game
- Fold early and block the player from winning
- Watch for disqualification opportunities

Whether you play in a private group that meets regularly or you play with a drop-in group:

1. Observe opponents within and across games.
2. Identify their playing styles:
   - Risk tolerance (assertive/passive)
   - Hand development (fixed/adaptive)
   - Hand selection (many/few, exposed/concealed, low value/high value)
3. Interpret their actions.
4. Adjust your tactics accordingly.

Savvy opponents will likely observe you, too, so try doing something counterintuitive from time to time to keep them off guard. For example, occasionally play like a dolphin even though you are a shark.

Also, players may use bluffing as a misdirection tactic. For example, a player may discard a natural tile in the middle-game instead of a joker, which would otherwise be a red flag that the player is ready to win on a single or pair tile.

Players can employ various maneuvers to counteract their opponents' tactics based on which stage the game is in. We will dig into tactics you can use when we cover "Hoptoi's Strategy by Wall" in the next chapter. For now just know that clues about playing styles differ depending on where you are in the game.

Practice profiling players and develop your critical thinking, situational awareness, and social acuity skills so you can use intel gathered to employ the right tactics at the right time in the game. This will give you an overall advantage at the table. Fine-tuning these skills takes time, so be patient with yourself and trust the process.

Now that we have covered how to play within the boundaries of the rules and how to use essential skills to your advantage, we are going to dig into some powerful strategies.

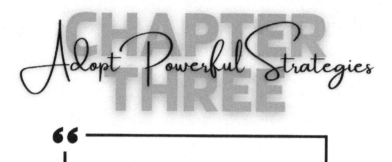

CHAPTER THREE

Adopt Powerful Strategies

> **THE SMARTER YOU PLAY**
> **THE LUCKIER YOU'LL BE**

Mark Pilarsky, gaming authority and author

Notes ...

Chapter 3: Adopt Powerful Strategies

There are more than 47 versions of mah jongg, and each contains elements that make it challenging and fun to play. In my opinion, American mah jongg is one of the most difficult versions to learn; however, once you learn the fundamentals, it's one of the easiest to play. To play well, you need to develop the essential skills covered in the previous chapter. To excel, you need to learn strategies and understand how to apply the tactics correctly.

Category Powers and Pitfalls

The hands on the card are divided into categories that, for the most part, stay the same from year to year. You can build your confidence in navigating the card by learning about the powers and pitfalls associated with each of its categories. Every year I analyze the League's new card, and I include a section on these powers and pitfalls in detail. You can find a link to my free e-book under downloads in the Mahj Life wiki article 162, "American Mah Jongg."

When your hand includes tiles that can be used for multiple categories, you will eventually need make a choice one way or the other. For example, one potential category may use most of your tiles while the other category may use most of your multiples. Another example might be that your tiles can be used in a category that has more hands or a category with greater flexibility. Because some categories use the same tiles, it is relatively easy to switch between them, allowing you to defer making a choice until you build more strength in one of them.

Year

Powers

- When you play in this category, you can thwart others from completing the big year hand, the highest value hand on the card (last hand in Singles-Pairs).

Pitfalls

- Hands require only two number tiles.
- Anyone playing an Evens hand can impact the availability of 2s and 4s.

Advice

- Consider this category if you have a strong representation of the year's tiles.
- Watch for White Dragons in discards and exposures.

Evens 2 4 6 8

Powers

- If you get odd tiles, you may have options in Consecutive Run.

Pitfalls

- Since there are gaps between even numbered tiles, switchability is limited.
- Fewer tiles might be available for this category if they are also needed for Year hands.

Advice

- Consider this category if you have gaps in your consecutive tiles or more multiples with even tiles than odd tiles.
- If you get odd tiles, consider switching to the Consecutive Run category, especially if you get 5s since they are the most efficient tile in the set.

Any Like Numbers

Powers	Pitfalls
• Depending on which hand you are focused on, you may be able to switch to another category containing hands with like numbers.	• Hands use only one number tile in mixed suits. • Sometimes, dragons and winds are included.

Advice

- There are usually two or three hands in this category but don't be deceived – there are like numbers all over the card.
- Passing like numbers will be almost as risky as passing a pair.

Math Play

Powers	Pitfalls
• These are typically Hands of Slight Resistance, which means if you have your flower pair in hand, you are able to complete the rest of the hand with the help of jokers, if necessary.	• Flowers are in every hand, and they may not be available. • Hands typically include singles or pairs.

Advice

- Math Play hands come and go on the NMJL card and usually show up as addition or multiplication.
- Have flowers in-hand before committing with more than one exposure.

Quints	

Powers	Pitfalls
• Use of big multiples (e.g., kongs, quints) so jokers can be very helpful.	• Exposures alert opponents that you are playing a high value hand.

Advice
• Consider this category if you have big multiples and at least one joker in your dealt hand, but the more jokers the better.

Consecutive Run	

Powers	Pitfalls
• Tile efficiency makes this a powerful category because it uses number tiles 1-9 in three suits with flexibility of a 5-number range.	

Advice
• Consecutive Run is the most powerful category on the card because hands use tiles numbered 1-9 in three suits. Also, they are efficient because you can move your starting number up or down if tiles you need become unavailable. If you choose to play a hand in this category and you have mixed suits, keep tiles in a four or five number range around your multiples or predominant pattern for the greatest flexibility.
• There are more consecutive run hands than any other type of hand, if you include hands in other categories that contain runs of consecutive numbers. If you are in between categories with equal potential, choose Consecutive Run.
• Consider starting your range so that your hand won't be affected by anyone playing a Year hand.
• Remember that despite the examples on the card starting at 1, you can start your run with any number unless the hand is followed by "these numbers only" in parentheses. There is no "around the world" in mah jongg, so be aware that your sequence cannot go beyond 9.

Odds

Powers	Pitfalls
• Hands use five numbers with options between little odds (1, 3, and 5) and big odds (5, 7, and 9).	• Since there are gaps between odd numbered tiles, switchability is limited.

Advice

- Consider this category if you have weak runs (e.g., gaps, singles) and have more odds than evens.
- If you get even tiles, consider switching to the Consecutive Run category especially if you get 4s and 6s since these – with the 5s – are the most efficient tiles in the set.

Winds - Dragons

Powers	Pitfalls
• There are typically hands that use consecutive runs.	• Options are limited. • There are typically very few hands outside the category, which means it has limited switchability.

Advice

- Consider this category if you have a strong representation of winds or dragons in your dealt hand.
- Monitor the number of winds being discarded in the begin-game. If winds go down early, carefully consider your choice of hands if you have gaps and weaknesses.
- If you pass winds during the Charleston, it is best to pass one at a time because there are hands with single winds. There are also hands with either North and South or East and West, so if you must pass two winds, try not to pass North and South or East and West together.
- Keep in mind that there are usually more hands on the card containing dragons than winds, so consider passing winds in the Charleston before passing dragons.

369

Powers	Pitfalls
• Hands use like numbers.	• Since there are gaps between the only three numbered tiles, switchability is extremely limited.

Advice
- Although the 369 category has a fair number of hands, it is not very flexible because it only uses three number tiles that have two-number spans between them, limiting your ability to switch categories. Therefore, make sure you have a good representation of 3,6,9 tiles before playing this category.
- If your hand does not develop by the middle-game, consider switching to Any Like Numbers if you don't have exposures or you have exposures that can be used.

Singles and Pairs

Powers	Pitfalls
• Hands have higher values. • Hands are concealed so they are switchable to other categories.	• Hands are shallow since they are comprised of singles and pairs. If you switch to a hand outside the category, it will require time to build the multiples.

Advice
- Consider this category if you have no jokers and few big multiples from the dealt hand.
- Hands typically align with another category on the card, such as Consecutive Run, Evens, or Odds. If you draw jokers, consider switching to another category before the middle of the game (e.g., 70 tiles remaining).

Most categories on the card contain two different types of hands, concealed and exposed, and each type also has powers and pitfalls.

Concealed hands require you to draw needed tiles from the wall to develop your hand to a ready status. When you are ready to win, you can declare mah jongg if your winning tile is discarded or if you pick your winning tile from the wall.

Powers	Pitfalls
• Without exposures, you stay in stealth mode • Hands are higher value • Can switch to an exposable hand if necessary; see summary in "Advice"	• Tiles needed for the hand can be discarded or used in exposures before the hand is ready to win

Advice
• Monitor weaknesses to help decide whether an exposable option has greater potential. • If you do not have singles and/or pairs needed for your hand by the middle-game (~60 tiles remaining), consider switching to an exposable hand. Look for options within the category that uses the same pattern as the concealed hand (e.g., Little Odds hands with pungs).

Exposed hands require you to pick tiles from the wall, but you can also claim discards to complete exposures.

Powers	Pitfalls
• Claiming discards for exposures can expedite hand development	• Hands are usually lower value • Each exposure deepens your commitment to a hand • Each exposure provides information to other players about your hand

Advice
• Stay concealed for as long as possible to maximize flexibility; with no exposures, you have the freedom to switch category, hand, type of hand, etc. • Monitor weaknesses to help decide whether you should switch to an option with greater potential.

Now that you have some insight into the powers and pitfalls for each category on the card, let's dig deeper by looking at hand development beginning with hand shapes.

Hand Shapes

When the league releases its new card, you will experience a period of adjustment that will be uncomfortable and can affect your confidence in playing the game. One solution is to memorize the prevalent shapes and patterns of the hands:

- The shape of a hand can be described by the blocks that make up the hand.
- The pattern of a hand can be described by the symbol tiles used to make up the hand.

Also consider that every hand on the card has a value that relates to the difficulty of completing it. For example, Quints have high values because they require jokers. Since any number of jokers can be used to complete these hands, they are low-risk hands. However, when you expose a quint, there is a good chance that one or more players will keep tiles to block you from winning, even if these players have to fold.

The highest risk hands are also worth the most. Singles and Pairs hands have the highest value because they consist of— you guessed it—singles and pairs. Hands containing more singles and pairs are riskier to play because most of the hands on the card use big multiples, such as pungs and kongs, and an opponent making one exposure with the tiles you need can destroy your hand. If you are playing a high-risk hand (three or more pairs required), always have a backup hand that you can switch in case your hand becomes unviable.

The card also contains two types of low-risk, low-value hand shapes. The first is any hand that requires two pungs and two kongs. I call these "hands of least resistance" because you can use any number of jokers to complete the hand, making them relatively indestructible.

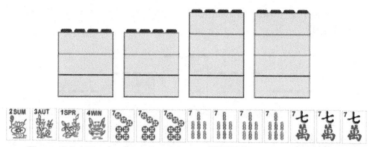

Figure 3.1.1 Hands of least resistance, MAMJ #Any Like Numbers #1

The second is any hand requiring one pair with big multiples. If the pair is already in your hand, you can use any number of jokers to complete the rest of the blocks, making the hand relatively indestructible. I call these "hands of slight resistance" (Fig. 3.1.2).

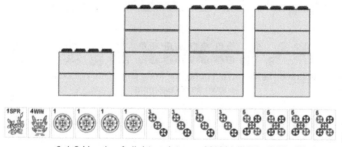

Figure 3.1.2 Hands of slight resistance MAMJ #Little Odds #3-1

Because these hands are relatively indestructible, they are great go-to hands. Keep in mind that these hands are only "relatively" indestructible because there is a slight chance that all eight jokers will eventually be locked in place and not available to you, such as when they are used in concealed hands, have been discarded, or when the natural tiles needed to exchange them in exposures have been discarded.

If you are torn between hands with equal potential and one is a hand of least or slight resistance, consider playing that hand. Also, consider playing these types of hands if you find yourself in a losing streak or if you are playing in a competitive event (Appendix B, "American Mah Jongg Skills and Strategies Matrix" [Mahj Life wiki article 210]).

Here are some other names for hands based on shape (Figs. 3.1.3-3.1.9):

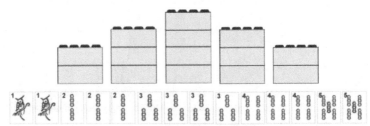

Figure 3.1.3 Pyramid Hands have a pair pung kong pung pair; MAMJ Consecutive Run #1

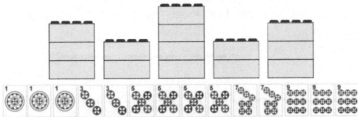

Figure 3.1.4 Castle Hands have a pung pair kong pair pung; not on the card but shown as an example

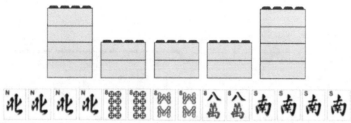

Figure 3.1.5 Gate Hands have big multiples with singles or pairs in the middle; MAMJ Winds-Dragons #4

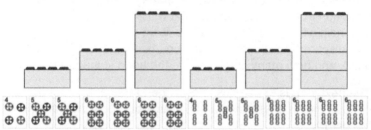

Figure 3.1.6 Double Run Hands have single pair kong using a three-tile sequence in two suits; not on the card but shown as an example

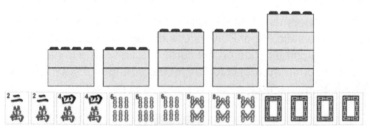

Figure 3.1.7 Step Hands have two pairs, two pungs, then a kong; MAMJ Evens #2

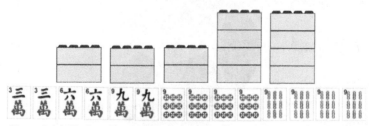

Figure 3.1.8 Big Step Hands have three pairs, then two kongs; MAMJ 369 #5

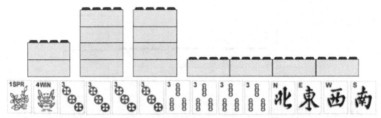

Figure 3.1.9 Trip Hands have an interrupted pattern with singles or little multiples; MAMJ Like Numbers #2

Knowing the shapes and patterns of the hands can help you transition from one card to the next with fewer mistakes. It can also help with hand choice and decision making during the pick-and-discard phase of the game (e.g., how many jokers can be used, and how many singles make the hand vulnerable).

The next step is to use this knowledge to transform your dealt hand to match the shapes and patterns of one of the hands on the card.

Hand Development

Hand development is the process of gathering useful tiles to complete a valid hand. Players use the tiles to create a hand that matches a combination on the card. The first stage in hand development (Fig. 3.2) is to **Target** the strength of your hand. In American mah jongg, a hand's power is in its multiples.

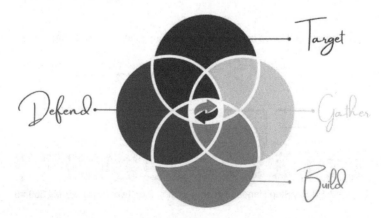

Figure 3.2 Phased Approach to Hand Development

After you receive your dealt hand, you can use one of two approaches. Since we play with a card listing valid hands, it is natural to want to pick a hand right away based on the tiles in your dealt hand. This method, as mentioned in the previous chapter, is called playing with a fixed approach. You can play this way, and it would not be wrong, but don't be surprised if you get stuck with a hand that is unviable later in the game. A flexible alternative is to pick a category based on the strength of your dealt hand and then **Gather** tiles that can be used for any hand in that category. Picking a hand is deferred until your hand only contains tiles that fit in this category. This method is called taking an adaptive approach because you have the freedom and flexibility to adapt your hand based on trends you observe as the game progresses.

Approximately 80% of the hands on the card use big multiples (e.g., pung, kong). To optimize your winning potential, look at your dealt hand and then choose a category that uses your multiples, especially bigger ones, and the tiles you have that support them. If you do not have multiples, identify the predominant pattern in your dealt hand, such as evens, odds, or 369, and then choose a category that uses the most of these tiles. When a multiple does form during the Charleston, reassess your tiles and choose a category that uses this multiple with supporting tiles. When all the tiles in your hand can be used in your chosen category, narrow down your hand options or even pick a specific hand.

Mah jongg is a flexible and forgiving game. You can make any hand work by making the right decisions at the right time. There is no right or wrong way to pick a hand, but there is a good, a better, and a best way (Fig. 3.3).

Figure 3.3 Fixed vs adaptive

Playing adaptively will require a paradigm shift if you currently play with a fixed approach. Here is how this change might look during gameplay:

> Arrange your dealt tiles in numerical order within each suit, and then group the jokers, flowers, winds, and dragons to give you an overview of your tiles.

> Target the strength of the hand, which will be either multiples or the predominant pattern (e.g., 2468, 13579, 369, Consecutive Run).

> Look at the remaining tiles and choose a category that uses the most of those tiles that support the strength of your hand.

> Identify clear discards. Clear discards are tiles that are not used in your chosen category. We will dig deeper into this concept in "Hoptoi's Strategy by Wall."

Target your multiples first and then look for tiles that can support these multiples. Focus on the category that uses most multiples and most of your tiles to support them. If your dealt hand does not contain any multiples, target the predominant pattern (e.g., mostly even numbered tiles, mostly odd numbered tiles) and focus on the category that uses most of your tiles.

Proceed through the Charleston until a multiple forms, and then reassess your tiles using that multiple. Next, whittle down your hand options within that category to free up tiles so that you can continue passing as defensively as possible during the remainder of the Charleston. Pick a hand when you have only tiles that can be used in your category (keepers), reassessing again when other multiples form.

In the begin-game, continue to gather supporting tiles to fill gaps in your hand and increase your options. Usually by the middle-game, you will see the potential for a couple of hands, and this is when you begin to **Build** multiples by keeping tiles and claiming discards to make exposures. Keep in mind that each exposure deepens your commitment to a hand because any hand you then play must include that exact exposure. We will go into greater detail with the stages of the game in the following sections.

Always remain aware of your opponents and **Defend** against them by surveying discards and monitoring exposures. Also remember that you may need to reassess your hand throughout the game to see if its potential has changed. If so, change your target and adjust the tiles you gather.

Hand development is a process that will take time to master. You can shorten your learning curve by practicing consistently and studying proven strategies.

Hoptoi's Strategy by Wall

Certain strategies in American mah jongg can maximize your potential for success in every game. Hoptoi's Strategy by Wall[9] falls into this category by narrowing your focus, encouraging critical thinking, and minimizing the likelihood that you will feel overwhelmed. The key to this strategy is compartmentalization.

---

[9] Hoptoi is my player name in online gaming platforms. Depending on the place where the wall is broken prior to dealing tiles to players, someone may receive the last stack of tiles in one wall and the first stack of tiles in the next wall. When this happens, the player says, "Hop toi," "I believe," as a declaration of magic or good luck being in those tiles (e.g., jokers, flowers, keepers). "Hop" means to shut in and "toi" means table, in other words, "keep the dragons (wanted tiles) inside the breached walls on the table."

compartmentalization

com·part·men·tal·i·za·tion /kəmˌpärtˌmen(t)ələˈzāSH(ə)n/

noun

GENERAL:

1) the division of something into sections or categories

Inspired by the stages in a chess game, Tom Sloper introduced the concept of adjusting tactics in American mah jongg based on the wall in play[10]. (Fig. 3.4.1-3.4.4).

Figure 3.4.1 The Charleston, 99 tiles remaining

---

[10] Sloper, Tom, (date not posted), Stages of the Game, https://sloperama.com/mjfaq/mjfaq08.htm

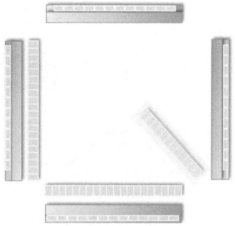
Figure 3.4.2 Begin-Game, 99-81 tiles remaining

Figure 3.4.3 Middle-Game, 80-41 tiles remaining

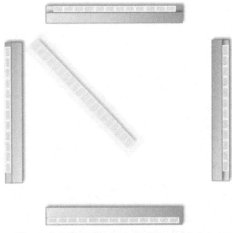

Figure 3.4.4 End-Game, 40-0 tiles remaining

Hoptoi's Strategy by Wall splits the game into four phases: pre-game, begin-game, middle-game, and end-game.

Pre-Game: The Charleston

When I learned how to play American mah jongg in 1990, I didn't like it. I felt confined when I played the game because of how the card limits the number of hands to choose from. After I studied the nuances of the game and figured out that I could adapt strategies and tactics from other mah jongg versions, such as Hong Kong Old Style and Riichi, as well as from card games such as poker and rummy, sparks began to fly. I began documenting my epiphanies that I am sharing with you in this book. I have already shared two of these epiphanies in the previous chapter and the third one has to do with the Charleston.

Since the game doesn't officially begin until East discards the first tile to start play, the Charleston can be considered a pre-game activity. This is when players attempt to transform their dealt hand in a series of passes to one another. If you harness the power of the Charleston, you can optimize your potential to win (Epiphany #3).

I am going to explain how to harness the power of the Charleston by breaking it into three segments:

The Purpose

The Power

The Promise

The Purpose

The Charleston provides you with your best opportunity during the game to expedite hand development because the series of passes from your opponents can involve up to 21 tiles in up to seven passes! Your primary objective each time you receive new tiles during the Charleston is to reassess and identify the strength of your hand. Choose a category that can use both the strength of your hand and as many of your other tiles to support it as possible.

expedite

ex·pe·dite /ˈekspəˌdīt/

verb

GENERAL:
1) to accelerate the process of or progress of; speed up

Focus: Improving your dealt hand

Situational Awareness: Remember both what types of tiles are and are not being passed.

Tactics:

Offensive Tactics for the Charleston
- Arrange tiles on your rack in the following order without spaces between the groups: jokers, flowers, winds, dragons, and each suit in numerical order.

- Identify and target the strength of the hand

  o Multiples are more powerful than single tiles; if you have multiples, choose a category that uses the majority of them and then keep tiles that can be used in that category, regardless of suit.

  o If you do not have multiples, look for the predominant pattern by visualizing or arranging your tiles by category and then select the category that uses the most tiles.

  o If the choice is still unclear, focus on the Consecutive Run category and keep tiles in a four or five number range around the strength of your hand, regardless of suit.

- Gather tiles for the category you are focusing on but resist the impulse to pick a specific hand and wait until the last possible moment to allow yourself the most flexibility; you do not need to pick a hand until you only have tiles that fit in your category.

- Reassess your hand after each pass, especially if a new multiple forms.

- Place tiles that you cannot use in your chosen category on one end of your rack; these tiles are your discards, while the others are your keepers. Remember not to leave a space between discards and keepers as this might give your opponents information about your hand.

- When you have only tiles that can be used in the category you a focusing on, look at the hands within the category to narrow down your options and free up more discards for any remaining Charleston passes. We'll dig deeper into this topic later in this chapter when we get to "Exercising Charleston Options."

Defensive Tactics for the Charleston
Mitigate risk in the tiles you are passing. Listed below are passing options from lowest to highest risk:

- A single wind or dragon with different number tiles of mixed suits.
- Different number tiles from each suit
- Tiles that can be used in the same category
- Tiles of the same suit
- White dragons or flowers (pass rarely)
- Like numbers are almost as risky as passing a pair, which you should only pass them as a last resort
- Pair (avoid passing)

Misdirection Tactics for the Charleston
An experienced player pays attention to how their opponents handle tiles from incoming passes. For example, are incoming tiles from this opponent placed on one end of the rack and then chosen for the next outgoing pass? If so, your opponent could glean information about the category you are playing by learning which tiles you do not keep. Therefore, when you receive a pass, put the tiles on your rack and then subtly shuffle them to prevent your opponents from detecting progress in your hand's development.

The Power

The power of the Charleston lies in the three tactics you can use when developing your hand: optimize, maximize, and streamline.

optimize

op·ti·mize /ˈäptəˌmīz/
verb

GENERAL:
1) to make as perfect, effective, or functional as possible

Figure 3.5.1 Target Multiples; Like Numbers with 7s
or Consecutive Run using big numbers

All American mah jongg hands contain combinations of pairs, pungs, or kongs. Therefore, target multiples to **optimize** hand development (Fig. 3.5.1).

If you don't have any multiples, you can find your hand's strength by identifying the predominant pattern in your tiles. When a multiple forms, target that multiple, reassess your hand, and gather tiles that support this multiple.

maximize

max·i·mize /ˈmaksəˌmīz/

verb

GENERAL:
1) to increase to a maximum

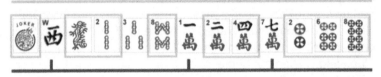

Figure 3.5.2 Choose a category that uses most of your tiles; Evens

Maximize your hand's potential by choosing the category that uses most of your tiles (Fig. 3.5.2).

streamline

stream·line /ˈstrēm-ˌlīn/

verb

GENERAL:
1) to design or construct with a streamline
2) to put in order
3) to make simpler or more efficient

Figure 3.5.3 Choose Consecutive Run using little numbers

If you are in between categories and one of the categories is Consecutive Run, **streamline** your options by choosing to focus on this category (Fig. 3.5.3).

Consecutive Run is the most flexible and efficient category on the card because you can change where in a run your hand begins, and the category offers plenty of hand options. Remember that hands containing consecutive runs also appear in other categories throughout the card.

Combine the tactics outlined above to make a **power play** and improve your starting position. Target multiples to **optimize** your potential, choose a category that uses the majority of your tiles to **maximize** possibilities, and play Consecutive Run hands to **streamline** your options.

Figure 3.5.4 Optimized by targeting multiples, maximized by using most of the tiles, and streamlined by choosing the Consecutive Run category

Handling Hot Commodities

Flowers are often coveted tiles in American mah jongg because they appear in nearly half of the hands on the card. For this reason, try not to pass flowers during the Charleston unless you know what hand you are playing, have no gaps in your hand, and do not have other tiles to pass instead. I think passing a flower is as risky as passing like numbers, both of which I consider one step less risky than passing a pair. Passing a pair should be a last resort used only if you are just one or two tiles away from being ready to win during the Charleston.

Dragons are also coveted tiles. Consider the risk of passing them as a close second to passing flowers. During the Charleston I tend to keep white dragons because they serve a dual purpose: they can function as either a dragon or as a zero in Year hands. If I have numbered tiles that I don't need, I will pass them with an unneeded wind before passing a white dragon.

Exercising Charleston Options

The Charleston consists of two rounds of three passes each, and it ends with a bonus optional across pass. The first round of a right, across, and left pass is compulsory, but the second round of left, across, right is optional. The bonus optional across pass at the end of the Charleston is negotiated between players. With each pass, players select three needless tiles to exchange with their opponents. Every pass entails some amount of risk, so just do your best to mitigate the risk by passing tiles that are less likely to work well together in a hand.

Players can take advantage of three additional options during the Charleston. These options should only be exercised after careful consideration to avoid alerting vigilant opponents to the level of hand development you have achieved. Let's look at the when, why, and how of each option.

Option One: Passing Blind

The first option is passing tiles blind in the last pass of each round, the first left and the second right passes. Passing blind allows you to supplement your outgoing pass with tiles from your incoming pass if you don't want to give away useful tiles from your hand. This process is called passing blind because you are not supposed to look at the incoming tiles before deciding which ones, if any, to include in your outgoing pass. There is no penalty if you peek at the tiles, but it is considered extremely bad form if you do.

If you are having difficulty deciding between categories or between hands, do not pass blind, as tempting as it may be. Instead, optimize and maximize by focusing on the strength of your hand to free up tiles to pass. Focus on the category that uses the most of your multiples. If you have no multiples, choose the category that uses the most of your tiles (Fig. 3.6).

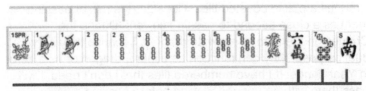

Figure 3.6 Between categories and hands: these tiles could be used in MAMJ Consecutive Run #1 or Little Odds #3 or #6

If you are between categories and one of the categories has a gap, choose the category with no gaps (Fig. 3.7).

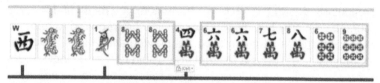

Figure 3.7 Gap-hand; There is potential for Evens but there are no 2s so choose the Consecutive Run category using 6789.

If you are committed to one hand and have fewer than three tiles you don't need, consider passing blind in the first left pass. Embrace the decision. It will be worth the risk if it results in a well-developed hand.

Option Two: Stopping the Second Charleston
Each player has the prerogative to stop the Charleston after the first left, no questions asked. The purpose of the second Charleston is to continue expediting hand development. Some players mistakenly believe that the second Charleston is a waste of time. Even though the second Charleston is optional, it's best to proceed under most circumstances because you will see up to 12 more tiles that could improve your hand. If your opponents do not feel they are making progress with their hand development or decide to pursue a different category based on the tiles they have received, they may change their hands and pass new tiles during the second Charleston. There may also be an opportunity for you to recover tiles you passed in the first round but now realize that you could use them.

Some players stop the second Charleston as a tactic to keep opponents from advancing their hand development. More often than not, though, that player is delaying their own hand development instead.

Do not stop the Charleston simply because you are between categories or between hands. Instead, optimize and maximize. Choose the category that uses the strength of your hand and has the most supporting tiles. If you are considering more than one category and there is a gap for one of the categories, choose the category with no gaps.

If you decide to stop the Charleston, don't be surprised if your opponent declines your offer in the optional across pass.

Particularly during the second Charleston, you might find yourself with only two discards when you are required to pass three tiles. In this situation, if you're playing a jokerless hand that contains singles, pass a tile that you would use as a single in the hand if possible. A single is easier to recover than a tile you need for a pair. If you are not playing a jokerless hand, pass a tile that you need for a big multiple because you can use a joker to replace it. If at all possible, do not pass a tile that would leave a gap in your hand. Even if you do not recover a sacrificed tile during the Charleston, you may be able claim a discard to complete an exposure with that tile or you may draw one from the wall.

If you're committed to one hand and only have three discards or fewer at the end of the first Charleston, stop the Charleston. Stopping the Charleston will alert your opponents that you likely have a well-developed hand, so consider being reactive in the optional across by waiting for your opponent to make an offer and then deciding if you want to participate.

Option Three: Courtesy or Optional Across Pass
The purpose of the courtesy or optional across pass is to provide a final chance to expedite hand development and, in some cases, recover useful tiles passed earlier in the Charleston. If your opponent stops the Charleston, they either have a well-developed hand or cannot decide which option to pursue. Therefore, you might decide against participating in the optional across pass so that you don't risk helping your opponent to build an even stronger hand. Be reactive in the negotiation to control information. If your opponent delays, ask if they want to pass any tiles, but don't make an offer yourself.

If someone ever says that they stopped the Charleston to keep their options open, they don't understand the purpose or the power of the Charleston.

Measuring Results
You can track your progress as you develop your Charleston skills by measuring results after the Charleston. Asking yourself

the right questions will allow you to assess your hand's transformation and estimate your position in the begin-game (Epiphany #4).

Envision a race-based arcade game at a county fair. The competitors are seated in front of a mechanical racetrack and the race begins. Some of the competitors are off and running. The competitors in the lead are frontrunners, while the competitors a few lengths behind are contenders. Competitors stuck behind the gates due to mechanical difficulties are underdogs. The game attendant adjusts the machine so that competitors stuck behind the gates can join the race.

Now consider that a game of mah jongg is like this race-based arcade game, but rather than running a race, the competitors are gathering tiles to be the first to complete a hand on the card. The players who made significant progress in developing their hands during the Charleston are the frontrunners. Players who made moderate progress are contenders, and players who made little to no progress in hand development are the underdogs.

To estimate your position in the game, you will need to assess the transformation of your hand after the Charleston. Ask yourself:

- Do you know what category you are focused on based on the strength of your hand?
- Do you know what hand you are playing?
- Do you have gaps?
- Do you have weaknesses?
- How many discards do you have?

Your position in the game and the level of risk you should take will depend on how you answer those questions.

If you have more than four discards, you are likely an **underdog** (Fig. 3.8.1). It's best to take a low-risk approach while you continue hand development. Do not claim discards for exposures until you know what hand you are playing, you have no gaps, and your hand has few weaknesses. If you are an underdog, take heart in knowing that you can come from behind with just a few good picks from the wall.

Figure 3.8.1 Underdog, Odd hand with five discards, MAMJ Odds #1-1

If you have four discards, you're likely a **contender** for that game. It's best to take a moderate-risk approach as you expedite hand development, calling for discards to make exposures once you know what hand you are playing, have no gaps, and have few weaknesses (Fig. 3.8.2).

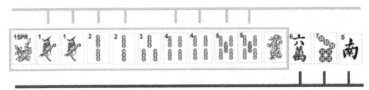

Figure 3.8.2 Contender, three discards and between MAMJ Consecutive Run #1-1 or Little Odd #3 or #6-1

If you have fewer than four discards, you're likely a **frontrunner** for that game (Fig. 3.8.3)! When you are this close to one or two hands, you can take risks. Expedite hand development by claiming discards to make exposures, even if it means you risk losing jokers in these early exposures.

Figure 3.8.3 Frontrunner, Like Number hand with two discards MAMJ, Like Numbers #1

Make a mental note of how often you are in the underdog position. If you feel you are not progressing to your liking during the Charleston, or if you want to fast track your improvement, consider working with a mentor (Appendix C).

The Promise

You will no longer struggle with the Charleston once you learn to harness its power. In practical terms, this means understanding and appreciating the purpose behind the process, applying tactics correctly and taking advantage of the opportunities to transform your dealt hand, and measuring the results by tracking your position. Remember that you can get help from an instructor if you are not progressing to your expectations.

The official start of the game is when East discards its first tile. You can continue hand development by picking one tile at a time from the wall. The next three sections will mention milestones that will teach you how to pace yourself throughout the game. Each number is a milestone that marks the number of tiles remaining in the wall.

Milestone	Phase in the game	Sweet spot
80	Beginning of the middle-game	Pick just one category
70	Early part of the middle-game	Switch hands
60	Middle of the middle-game	Pick just one hand; discard joker bait
50	Late part of the middle-game	Gather safe discards
40	Beginning of the end-game	Decide whether to push to win or to fold

Begin-Game

The begin-game starts after the Charleston (99 tiles remaining). From this point on, the level of risk you are willing to accept when making decisions should be based on your position in the game—underdog, contender, or frontrunner. If you draw well, your position can change from underdog to contender or from contender to frontrunner. Choose your tactics wisely as you continue to develop your hand and remember to apply situational awareness and social acuity skills to gather intel and make informed decisions.

Focus: Gather tiles to support the strength of your hand.

Situational Awareness: You may be able to claim discards for exposures to expedite hand development. However, just because you can claim a discard does not necessarily mean you should. Every exposure deepens your commitment to a hand and provides your opponents with information. You need to assess these risks before deciding. Consider the following when deciding whether to claim a discard for an exposure:

Your hand's standing based on:

- The phase of the game
- The number of picks you have remaining in the wall (divide total tiles remaining by four)
- The number of discards in your hand
- The number of tiles you need that are visible in discards and exposures
- The progress of your opponents' hands based on their exposures

Then ask yourself:

- Do I know what hand I'm playing?
- Does my hand have no gaps?
- Does my hand have fewer than three weaknesses?

Asking yourself these questions can help you determine your position in the game and the level of risk you can take. If the answer to all three questions is yes, claiming a discard to complete an exposure is low risk. If the answer to any of these questions is no, claiming a discard to make an exposure is high risk. Accept the risk and claim the discard to make an exposure or don't claim the discard and, instead, continue gathering tiles for your category.

The primary advantage of claiming a discard to make an exposure is that you expedite your hand's development. Another reason to claim a discard, though, might be to block an opponent's hand development. Either way, the primary disadvantage of claiming a discard is visibility. Advanced players can identify the category or hand you are playing by monitoring exposures and surveying discards.

The potential negative ramifications of delaying exposures include needing a joker to complete that exposure or potentially needing to switch your hand to another option. If you are playing a hand of least or slight resistance, you may be able to recover with jokers.

Expediting hand development is crucial to staying ahead of your opponents. However, making an early exposure can diminish a hand's options and reveal intel. Consider the risks of these decisions before making them (Fig. 3.9).

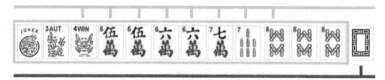

Figure 3.9 Delay exposure— in-between hands with equal strength so wait.
MAMJ Consecutive Run #2 and #3

fear of missing out

FO·MO /'fōmō/

noun

IN GENERAL:
1) concern that an interesting event may currentl

IN MAH JONGG:
1) anxiety of losing jokers in an early exposure
2) anxiety that opportunities for hand developme

calculated risk

cal·cu·lat·ed risk /'kalkyə‚lādəd/ /risk

adjective

IN GENERAL:
1) a risk that you consider worth taking because tl
so good or too good to pass up

Don't calculate risk based on FOMO. Instead, calculate risk based on intel gathered by reading the room. Reading the room includes reading hands and reading your opponents' behaviors. Also survey discards and note early exposures that may impact your hand development so that you can switch categories or hands when necessary.

Tactics:

Offensive Tactics for the Begin-Game

- Stay concealed for as long as possible.
- Play at the category level for as long as possible.
- Reassess your hand if a new multiple forms.
- Check that you are not playing a concealed hand before calling for a discard.
- Claim a discard only if you know what hand you are playing and your hand has no gaps and few weaknesses.
- Narrow your hand options to one category by the beginning of the third wall (Milestone 80).

Defensive Tactics for the Begin-Game

- Watch the first five rounds of discards to identify which categories your opponents are likely not playing.

Misdirection Tactics for the Begin-Game

- Handle needless tiles picked from the wall differently every few turns to keep your opponent's guessing about your hand's development. For example, if you are playing big odds (579) and you draw a 6, shuffle it around on your rack and discard a different tile so that it will appear that your pick was a keeper.
- If you have no discards aside from the tile you just picked, shuffle the new tile with a few other tiles on your rack before discarding it.

Look for red flags:

- Exposures, especially early in the game, could indicate a well-developed hand.
- Discarding jokers could indicate that an opponent is playing a Singles and Pairs hand or needs a tile to complete a pair.

Planning Discards in the Begin-Game

Planning discards is an important task that can help you simplify decision-making, optimize the potential for joker exchanges, and sabotage your opponents' hands. Potential discards will depend on your chosen category or hand. For example, if you are not playing winds, those tiles are useless, and you should discard them first. If you are not playing dragons, they are not only useless, but they can also increase in risk as the game progresses. Discard them next. In general, you should identify and prioritize discards as follows:

Useless tiles (depending on your chosen category; fig 3.10.1)

- Winds
- Dragons
- Year tiles
- Extraneous tiles (e.g., you're playing a hand in the Evens category, discard odd tiles)

Figure 3.10.1 Clear Discards (in this case useless tiles and a needless pair) with Joker Bait, MAMJ Consecutive Run #2

Misfit tiles (tiles that can be used in your category but not the hands you are focused on; Figure 3.10.2)

- Isolated tiles
- Redundant tiles

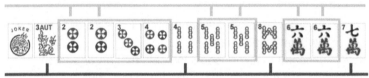

Figure 3.10.2 Clear Discards (in this case the 8 bam is an isolated and the 4 bam is a redundant tiles), MAMJ Consecutive Run #6

Outside-In

Outside-In (Epiphany #5) is a tactic for prioritizing discards during the begin-game and the middle-game. The theory is based on there being fewer hands that use winds and dragons than use number tiles and, therefore, number tiles are more likely to show up in exposures with jokers. Additionally, Consecutive Run is the most flexible category on the card, so there is a higher chance of one or more players choosing hands in that category. Opponents playing Consecutive Run are likely to use tiles in the middle of 1–9 rather than at either end because you can move the number range up or down based on tiles picked or thrown. Therefore, discard 1s and 9s, then 2s and 8s, then 3s and 7s if you are not playing a hand that uses those tiles (Fig. 3.11.1).

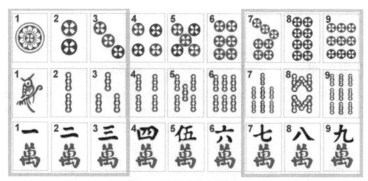

Figure 3.11.1 Outside-In

Discarding these tiles leaves the most efficient tiles in your hand for joker exchanges (Fig. 3.11.2).

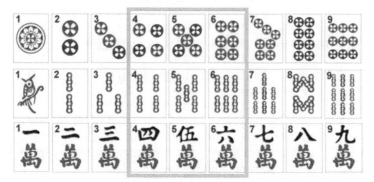

Figure 3.11.2 Most efficient tiles

If a player discards a tile that you are keeping in the hope of a joker exchange and no one claims it, you should discard this tile next because your opponents are likely not playing them. Also, if you are holding an efficient tile that is discarded by another player and someone claims it to make an exposure with a pure pung (i.e., no jokers), discard that tile next because it holds no purpose.

As you gather tiles for your chosen category, monitor discards and exposures for needed tiles to assess each hand's potential. Three indicators, in particular, can provide additional insight into which category or hand you might want to play:

- Category tiles: You are focused on the Evens category, and an opponent exposes 2s needed for several of these hands. Consider switching to the Consecutive Run category by holding odd tiles in your number range.

- Proximity tiles: You are focused on the Consecutive Run category, and an opponent exposes a pung of 7s and a kong of 9s. Another opponent is discarding 8s. Consider gathering tiles 1 through 6 since your opponents are using or have discarded 7s, 8s, and 9s.

- Like numbers: You are focused on the Year category and an opponent discards a white dragon, but you are not ready to claim it to make an exposure. Consider switching to the Consecutive Run category by gathering tiles that create a run with your Year tiles.

If your tiles are being discarded and you're not ready to act on them, or if your opponents make exposures using your tiles, consider switching to something with greater potential, especially if your hand has gaps or weaknesses.

It's okay to consider hands in a couple of categories while picking from the second wall. Don't straddle categories for too long, though, because eventually you need to focus on hands in one category. It's ideal to focus on one category by the beginning of the second wall (Milestone 80, One Category Sweet Spot).

Middle-Game

The middle-game occurs when the third wall is in play (80-41 tiles remaining).

Focus: Hand development and heightened situational awareness.

If you have not been able to make progress with hand development quickly enough, your position can change from frontrunner to contender or from contender to underdog. Adjust the level of risk you are willing to accept accordingly.

Situational awareness: Survey discards and monitor exposures to determine which categories your opponents are likely to be focused on.

The early part of the middle-game, ~80-60 tiles remaining, is the sweet spot for picking a hand. As you look at your options, consider:

- Switchability: options should use two or more common tiles.
- Dependency: options must use your current exposures, if any.
- Feasibility: options should have few tiles in discards or other players' exposures.

Tactics:

Offense in the Middle-Game

- Watch what other players are discarding and exposing to identify their categories and adjust your strategy accordingly.
- If you need to switch to another hand, try to do it in the early part of the middle wall (Milestone 70, Switch Sweet Spot).
- Discard joker bait; 60 tiles remaining is the ideal time for this tactic (Milestone 60, Joker Bait Sweet Spot).

- Redeem jokers from another player's rack but leave at least one joker in their exposures to avoid making their hand jokerless (double value).

Defense in the Middle-Game

- Survey opponents' discards and monitor exposures to confirm their focus.
- It's ideal to pick a hand by the middle of the third wall (Milestone 60 Pick One Hand Sweet Spot).
- It's ideal to be ready to win by the end of the third wall.
- Pay special attention to post-exposure discards. They can provide further information about the rest of that opponent's hand.
- Discard risky tiles and hold safer discards three picks from the end of the third wall (Milestone 50, Safe Discards Sweet Spot).
- If you are using the Outside-In discard tactic, switch to Inside-Out (Fig. 3.11.3) towards the end of the third wall because, in the end-game (last 40 tiles), it is important to keep safe discards, such as tiles that have already been discarded or are in exposures, for the final phase of the game (fourth wall).

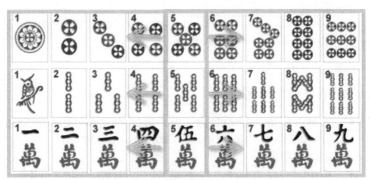

Figure 3.11.3 Tile Efficiency, Inside-Out

Misdirection Tactics in the Middle-Game

- Be mindful of your own post-exposure discards. If possible, discard a tile that will not reveal the category you are playing. For example, if you are playing big odds and expose a pung of 7 dots, discard a 3 crak instead of any 6s or 8s that you could also discard.

Look for red flags:

- Opponents making exposures.
- Opponents discarding jokers.

During the middle-game, your hand options may be within the same category or across different categories. Either way, stay concealed for as long as possible. The moment you claim a discard for an exposure, you limit your options. After two exposures, you are typically committed to one hand and your opponents can likely figure out what hand you are playing.

When comparing opportunities, whether they are within one category or across different categories, focus on hands where you don't have any gaps. When choosing a hand to play, any opportunity with a gap should take lower precedence. Also, try not to commit to a hand if you have any gaps, especially if the gap is a pair (Fig. 3.12).

Figure 3.12 Gap-hand, predominantly odds in one suit but 5 craks are missing, MAMJ Odds #1

Expediting Hand Development

One way to expedite hand development is to play an open (exposable) hand. Remember, however, that when you claim a discard to make an exposure, you are giving your opponents information. The more exposures you have, the easier it is for your opponents to determine what hand you are playing. Consider your position in the game to confirm whether you should be taking this risk in the middle-game.

The following situations could put you at risk of not completing your hand and should make you think twice about claiming discards to make an exposure:

- Gaps: You have one or more missing components in your hand.
- Weaknesses: You have one or more "shallow" components, an inadequate quantity of a tile for a big multiple, in your hand.
- Vulnerability: The tiles you need have been discarded or are in exposures, either of which can put you at risk.

If you don't know what hand you are playing, you are an underdog. If you do know what hand you are playing but your hand has gaps and weaknesses, you are likely an underdog. In either case, it's best to take a low-risk approach while you continue to develop your hand with tiles picked from the wall. Do not claim discards for exposures until you know what hand you are playing and have no gaps and few weaknesses.

If you know what hand you are playing and have no gaps and few weaknesses, you're likely a contender. It's best to take a moderate-risk approach as you expedite hand development by claiming discards to make exposures.

If you know what hand you are playing and have no gaps or weaknesses, you're likely a frontrunner, so you can take risks. Expedite hand development by claiming discards to make exposures.

That said, it's best to minimize your exposures to make it more difficult for your opponents to detect what hand you are playing. This is what I call **stealth mode** (no exposures) or **semi-stealth mode** (one exposure). To have the best chance of remaining in stealth or semi-stealth mode, obtain as many jokers as you can.

Joker Tactics

One of the differentiators in American mah jongg is its use of eight jokers. These tiles are needed in this version because the annual card has a limited selection of hands, and the players vie for the same tiles. If jokers were not included, most games would end in a draw.

So how do you obtain jokers other than picking them from the wall? You use tactics to increase your opportunities for a joker exchange.

Review the **Outside-In** tactic described in "Planning Discards in the Begin-Game" because this tactic supports the strategy of increasing the likelihood of obtaining jokers.

Joker bait, a term coined by Tom Sloper[11], is a hit-or-miss tactic for increasing your chances of obtaining a joker through a joker exchange. Joker bait takes advantage of the fact that approximately 80% of the hands on the American mah jongg card use big multiples, so there is a high likelihood that players will claim discards to make exposures to expedite completing their hands. Some of those exposures might have jokers, and players with the natural tile the joker represents have the option of exchanging that tile for the joker during their turn (Fig. 3.13; a red box identifies joker bait). Note that flowers rarely make good joker bait. With eight flower tiles in a set, another player is likely to make the exchange before you have the chance.

---

[11] Sloper, Tom, 9/13/2009, Joker Bait,
https://www.sloperama.com/mahjongg/column423a.htm

Figure 3.13 Joker bait (holding a needless pair, dragons) , MAMJ Winds-Dragons
#2

Here is how joker bait works:

1. During the Charleston you may have a needless pair
   that you might use as joker bait, but it can be an
   encumbrance to developing your hand. If you have less
   than three tiles to pass, consider breaking up the joker
   bait so you can pass fully and not sacrifice a needed tile.

2. After the Charleston, if you end up with a needless pair,
   keep it.

3. In the middle of the game (~60 tiles remaining), discard
   one of the paired tiles to coax an exposure with a joker.

4. If another player claims the discard and makes an
   exposure with a joker, make a joker exchange on your
   next turn with the other tile.

If, before you discard your first joker bait tile, another player
discards the same tile and no one calls it, it is unlikely that
anyone needs that tile for their hand. Discard these tiles as soon
as possible.

Now that you know how to optimize the potential for exchanging jokers, when to do a joker exchange is situational. If you have an opportunity to exchange a joker, do it if you can benefit from the following situations:

- The exchange will improve your potential to win
- The exchange will block another player from doing an exchange later
- The exchange will likely not result in the player winning with a pure hand because they have other exposure(s) with jokers
- The exchange will allow you to discard the joker instead of discarding the natural tile that could be the winning tile for another player

Finesse

When you are waiting or ready to win, there is one more joker tactic that may allow you to declare a self-picked win. **Finesse**, a term coined by Ruth Unger, is a tactic in which you can use a joker exchange for a self-picked win, which doubles the value of your hand.

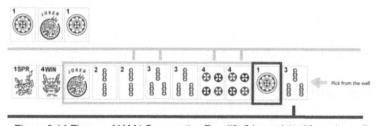

Figure 3.14 Finesse, MAMJ Consecutive Run #3; 3 bam picked from the wall

Here's how it works: You claim a discard and make an exposure with a joker. Later in the game you draw the natural tile but you keep it so you can use it to exchange the joker in your exposure and use the joker as your winning tile (Fig. 3.14). When you either claim a discard to make a final exposure or draw a keeper, you use the natural tile to exchange it for your joker and then use the joker to complete another concealed block and declare mah jongg.

Planning Discards in the Middle-Game

At 50 tiles remaining, you should stop using Outside-In to prioritize your discards so that you can prepare for the end-game. Your discard plans will now depend on how likely you are to win. Analyzing whether to push to win or fold your hand is covered in more detail in this chapter's discussion of the end-game. For now, suffice to say that, if the situation with your hand and what you see at the table suggest either that you are a frontrunner or a contender, you should now switch to discarding tiles Inside-Out. Remember that the most efficient tiles, 4–6 (Fig. 3.11.3), are likely to be tiles other players need. That is why those tiles are more likely to be used in exposures during the middle-game. However, as you near the end of the game, those tiles are increasingly likely to be an opponent's winning tile. If you are still playing to win, you want to rid your hand of these and other high-risk tiles and hold tiles that will be safer to discard during the end-game. Other high-risk tiles include unseen tiles (tiles that have not appeared in discards or exposures), dragons (especially white dragons), and flowers. Safer tiles are the ones you see in discards and exposures.

If you are an underdog and you decide that your better option is to fold, your only goal is to avoid discarding another player's winning tile. Hold risky tiles and break up your hand to free up more safe tiles for discards.

End-Game

The end-game begins when players start picking tiles from the fourth wall (~40 tiles remaining).

Focus: Greater situational awareness and heighted defense.

Situational Awareness: Continually assess the viability of your hand by surveying discards and monitoring exposures and then making decisions based on whether you should push to win or fold.

Tactics:

Offense in the End-Game

Unless you have already broken up your hand, reassess your position. If you decide that you are still playing to win, continue prioritizing your riskiest tiles for discards. If you decide to fold, break up your hand to free up safer tiles for discards and hold risky tiles instead.

When you are one or two tiles away from a winning hand, assess the likelihood of receiving the tiles you need by considering the following variables:

- The number of picks that remain in the wall
- The number of your winning tile in discards or exposures
- The number of your opponents' likely winning tiles in your hand, discards, or exposures
- The values of your opponents' likely hands

Defense in the End-Game

- If you draw a risky tile, consider the likelihood that discarding it could give an opponent mah jongg and whether that risk is acceptable.

Misdirection in the End-Game

- If you are not playing a pure (jokerless) hand and you have jokers, discard a natural tile instead of a joker so that you don't persuade your opponents to fold.

Look for red flags:

- Opponents' post-exposure discards can be telling if they have other exposures and if you have been keeping track of their other discards.
- Opponents making exposures are likely to have a strong potential to win.
- Opponents discarding jokers can indicate that a player is waiting for a single or pair tile, but it can also indicate that a player has decided to fold.

Wait Patterns

When you are waiting for the last tile to complete your hand, your hand has something called a wait pattern. Below are wait patterns listed from weakest to strongest:

A single wait means that your hand is missing a specific tile that is used as a single (Fig. 3.15.1).

Figure 3.15.1 Single wait, MAMJ 369 #6

A pair wait means that your hand is missing one tile to complete a pair. A "naked wait" is when you have only one concealed tile so everyone knows you are waiting to complete a block of two single tiles or a tile to complete a pair. Try to avoid this type of a wait (Fig. 3.15.2).

Figure 3.15.2 Pair wait, MAMJ Winds-Dragons #2

A multiple wait means that you need either a natural tile or a joker to complete a big multiple (Fig. 3.15.3).

Figure 3.15.3 Multiple wait, MAMJ Like Numbers #1

A double wait means that you need one of two natural tiles or a joker to complete one of two big multiples (e.g., pung, kong) because you have at least one joker in your hand that can be reallocated to complete the other multiple (Fig. 3.15.4).

Figure 3.15.4 Double wait, MAMJ Evens #2

A triple wait means that you need one of three natural tiles or a joker to complete one of three big multiples (e.g., pung, kong) because you have at least one joker in your hand that can be reallocated to complete the other multiples (Fig. 3.15.5).

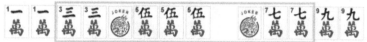

Figure 3.15.5 Triple wait, MAMJ Odds #1

A quad wait means that you need one of four natural tiles or a joker to complete one of four big multiples (e.g., pung, kong) because you have at least one joker in your hand that can be reallocated to complete the other multiples (Fig. 3.15.6).

Figure 3.15.6 Quad wait, MAMJ Consecutive Run #2

Your potential to win is proportionate to the strength of your wait (Fig. 3.15.7). This is why obtaining jokers is so exciting especially at this part of the game. You can reallocate jokers to fill in for more than one tile to complete two or more multiples.

WAIT PATTERNS					
Single	Pair	Multiple	Double	Triple	Quad
Weak		Strong	Stronger		Strongest

STRENGTH

Weak ← → Strong

POSITION

Underdog ← Contender → Frontrunner

Figure 3.15.7 Wait patterns

In the end-game, you need to manage your expectations by estimating your potential to win. Here are examples of how positions can be adjusted (e.g., 40 tiles remaining).

East has been a frontrunner for the entire game, but one of their needed tiles was just discarded and they couldn't claim it. They should bump back to a contender and take minimal risks or fold if they draw risky discards (Fig. 3.16.1).

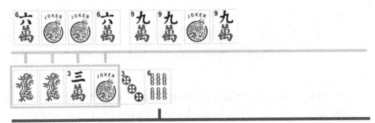

Figure 3.16.1 East position, MAMJ 369 #1

South has been a contender for most of the game, and they are playing a pair hand so they are fully concealed. They still need need a 4 crak and an East so they should bump back to underdog and consider folding (Fig. 3.16.2).

Figure 3.16.2 South position, MAMJ Singles and Pairs #1 with two discards

West has been an underdog the entire game. They need a North for NEWS and a 4 crak. Since North is playing a quint, West should stay as an underdog and fold (Fig. 3.16.3).

Figure 3.16.3 West position, MAMJ Evens #6 with one discard

North has been a contender most of the game. A joker in one of their exposures is available for exchange. The tile they are waiting for was discarded in the middle-game, but they weren't ready to claim it. They just drew a joker, making them ready to win, so they should bump up to frontrunner and push to win (Fig. 3.16.4).

Figure 3.16.4 North position, MAMJ Quints #1 with a Multiple Wait

Take both your position in the game and your wait pattern into account as you assess potential risks with each pick and discard.

Risk Assessment

Use this Risk Assessment Matrix (Fig. 3.17) to help you determine the probability and the impact of your discards. Visualize it when you play to help you decide the level of risk you are willing to accept.

RISK ASSESSMENT MATRIX			Impact			
			Acceptable	Tolerable	Unacceptable	Intolerable
			Opponent has no exposures	Opponent has one exposure	Opponent has two exposures	Opponent has three exposures
Likelihood	Improbable	Risk unlikely to occur	Low	Medium	Medium	High
	Possible	Risk likely to occur	Low	Medium	High	Extreme
	Probable	Risk most likely to occur	Medium	Medium	High	Extreme

Figure 3.17 Risk Assessment Matrix

The likelihood that your discard could allow another player to declare mah jongg is based on how many of their needed tiles have been discarded or exposed. For example, if you have an unwanted tile in the end-game and there are three of the same tiles in the discard area, the tile was never called by another player so it is probably safe to discard.

The impact of a discard will depend on another player's readiness and their number of exposures. If you discard an unwanted tile that results in an opponent declaring mah jongg, you will incur a penalty (e.g., double the hand's value). The impact on a player when they discard a risky tile in a competitive game can be even greater (e.g., with two exposures, discarder incurs a penalty of -20 points, with three exposures, discarder incurs a penalty of -25 points).

Push-Fold Judgment

At the beginning of the end-game (Milestone 40, Push-Fold Judgment), you will need to make a judgment call on whether to push to win or to fold with each pick and discard. Your challenge will be to estimate your potential to win, assess the risks, and decide what to do from there. If you decide to fold, you will need to break up your hand and discard safely. If you push to win, you will need to accept the consequences of discarding a risky tile.

Keep in mind that players estimate their potential to win and perceive risks differently. For example, if someone were to look at your hand in the end-game, they may tell you what you should or should not do based on their experience in the game and their playing style. The challenge for opponents and onlookers is to accept that judgment calls are subjective. Just like beauty, *should* is in the eye of the beholder.

Push Judgment
If you think your winning tile is in the wall or that an opponent might discard it, push to win (Fig. 3.18.1).

Figure 3.18.1: Push to win; you have only one discard and a potential double wait, MAMJ Addition #1-1

Tactics:

- Discard the riskiest tile first so you have safer tiles to discard as the game progresses.

- Reassess every picked tile from the wall especially if another player makes exposures, because they are pushing to win too and may have a stronger wait.

Fold Judgment
If you think the chances of getting your winning tile are slim, fold (Fig. 3.18.2).

Figure 3.18.2: Fold; flowers are risky discards because they are in almost half the hands and
white dragons are also risky discards because many times they are used as singles, MAMJ 369 #4-2

Tactics:

- Keep risky tiles, break up your hand, and discard as safely as possible to force a wall game (draw).

- Do not claim discards for exposures because exposures give other players valuable information.

- Discard tiles that have been exposed or previously discarded; the safest tiles to discard are ones where the other three tiles are already out (except for Year tiles and Math-Play singles).

- Discard jokers but save them to be your last discards because they are the only truly safe discards.

Applying Tactics

For any strategy to succeed, you need to apply its tactics correctly. One critical factor often determines how successful your tactics will be: timing. Intel gathered through situational awareness and social acuity can help you decide what the optimal time is for executing tactics. For example, there are more and less appropriate times to use joker bait:

Too early: A player holds joker bait during the Charleston for use in the middle-game. In this case, the tactic of holding joker bait is applied too early. Holding joker bait during the Charleston means having fewer tiles for passes, hindering the player's ability to develop their hand.

Too late: A player holds joker bait until the end-game. In this case, discarding these tiles increases in risk with every round because opponents have had more opportunities to develop their hands and could need only one of those tiles to win that late in the game.

Just right: A player develops an unneeded pair in the begin-game and holds it to use as joker bait in the middle-game. That player discards one of those tiles with about 60 tiles remaining in the wall. An opponent calls the discard to complete an exposure with a joker. On the player's next turn, they exchange the second tile for the joker. SUCCESS!

It will take time to integrate these powerful tactics into your playing style. You will need to play lots of mah jongg to learn how to apply them with the proper timing, so take advantage of every opportunity to play in-person and online. Be patient with yourself and trust the process.

CHAPTER FOUR

Maintain a Healthy Mindset

"

SUCCESS
IS ON THE OTHER SIDE OF GRIT

"

Unknown

Notes ...

Chapter 4: Maintain a Healthy Mindset

Playing mah jongg should be enjoyable for everyone at the table, but mah jongg is a challenging and sometimes exasperating game. How can you learn from every game yet avoid feeling frustrated when you lose? By maintaining a healthy mindset!

"It's not whether you win or lose, it's how you play the game" is derived from Grantland Rice's poem 'Alumnus Football'.[12] He wrote to encourage athletes to enjoy competition, put forth their best effort, and focus more on the process than on the outcome. Mah jongg is not a physical sport, but it is a mind sport, so this concept still applies. Your attitude directly impacts your ability to focus, which can affect your performance and ultimately shape your experience. By training yourself to keep a clear mind, challenges will not throw you off course so easily.

Attitude is a choice. Your attitude manifests in your emotions and your behavior, both of which you can control. You decide how to perceive what happens around you and how you will respond.

Consider adopting the following courtesies I've learned over decades of playing with countless groups:

Prior to Game Day

- Know the group culture.
- Know the rules of the game, including any house rules.
- RSVP and show up or cancel with enough notice for the group to find another player.

The Preliminaries

- Take your own tiles during the game. Unless asked, do not touch other players' tiles.
- Leave your tiles face down until the dealing is complete.
- Leave the broken wall in its original place to the far right of the rack.

---

[12] Rice, Grantland, 1908, https://tinyurl.com/yt7mncs3

The Charleston

- Wait to give another player an outgoing pass until after all players have their previous incoming pass in their hands.
- Announce the second left and ask if everyone wants to continue.
- Do not question a player who stops the Charleston before the second round of passes.

The Play

- Clearly name your discarded tile.
- Push the active wall forward as it depletes so that everyone can reach it.
- Offer joker exchange tiles hand to hand.
- In exposures, bookend jokers with natural tiles when possible.
- Separate exposures on your rack so that they are clearly delineated.
- Keep comments about the game in play to yourself.

The Pay

- If you win, arrange your tiles as they appear on the card then announce the winning hand with the value. This way, your opponents can validate the hand and reward you accordingly.
- If an opponent wins, do not throw in your tiles until the hand has been verified. After a win is verified, congratulate, and pay the winner.
- If you folded, refrain from showing off the risky tiles you kept preventing your opponents from winning.
- Avoid commiserating about what happened in the game.

Good sportsmanship and etiquette are subjective, but some examples of questionable behavior during a game might include too much chatting, discussing one's hand, complaining, and criticizing. To paraphrase The Golden Rule, "Treat others as you want to be treated." Following are nine ways to be the player you would want to play with:

Be patient: Mah jongg is a complex game and, from time to time, we may need to take a moment to make decisions about a discard. A guideline recommended by the League is to pause a beat before picking a tile from the wall or claiming a discard. To quantify pausing a beat, a common rule-of-thumb is to count to three.

Be Kind: Analyzing or criticizing another player's choices can cause hard feelings. Bite your tongue, focus on yourself, and share advice only when asked.

Silence is golden: Constant chatter during a game can make it hard to concentrate. Feel free to talk while mixing the tiles, but keep conversation to a minimum during the game unless the group you play with is particularly social.

Mind your manners: We all appreciate the convenience of using mobile devices, especially if we have family members who need to stay in touch. At a minimum, put your device on silent. Consider checking for messages between games and request to take a break if an urgent matter arises.

Mind your tells: Running commentary about each pass, pick, or discard will irritate many players. Not only that, but the commentary can also give away valuable information to your opponents, which can impact your potential to win. Avoid talking about gameplay. For example, don't comment when a joker is discarded or when a natural tile is discarded but could have been used for a joker exchange.

Respect personal space: For many players, their rack is their castle to be defended against foes. Joker exchanges are best done hand to hand. If you want to do a joker exchange, first verbalize the request. Then hand the natural tile to the player who has the joker exposed. The League recommends that a player not place the natural tile or the joker on the table or touch another player's tiles.

Respect the tiles: At times our emotions can get the better of us, and we might take our frustration out on the tiles. Handling the tiles with tender loving care is appreciated by the other players and the owner of the set, especially when playing with a vintage or designer set. Also, consider taking a break from the game to eat so that you can nosh away from the tiles and keep the table tidy and the tiles clean.

Maintain dignity in victory or defeat: Commiserating with other players after a game may seem harmless, but doing so can dampen the mood of other players at the table. Win with humility, lose with grace, and do both with dignity.

When in Rome: The League publishes guidelines and rulings in "Mah Jongg Made Easy," and most groups adhere to them. Playing by the official rules maintains fairness and ensures the integrity of the game. To enliven the game, some groups add house rules that are not in the booklet. When playing with a new group, always ask about any house rules ahead of time and adjust your style of play accordingly.

If you follow these guidelines, you will likely enjoy the game more. Not only that, but you will also be a joy to play with.

How to Handle a Losing Streak

losing streak

lo·sing streak /ˈlo͞oziNG/ /ˈstreak/

noun

GENERAL:
1) an uninterupted string of games lost by an individual
2) a winless streak; includes wall games and abandoned games

When playing a complex game like mah jongg, it's important to keep a clear head. On occasion, your mindset can be affected by losses, which can take the fun out of the game for both you and others. When you find yourself in that situation, here are four ways to check your thoughts and adjust your mindset.

Reality Check

With four players at the table, you might expect that you should win around 25% of the games. However, that expectation is unrealistic for several reasons.

First, wall games are not unusual and will affect your win rate.

Second, the people you play with and the format can change the dynamics of the game.

Third, mah jongg is a skill-based game with an element of luck. It has even been included in the *List of World Championships in Mind Sports*[13].

Many strategy games include varying degrees of luck. I've heard some people say that American mah jongg is 75% luck and 25% skill. In my opinion, the outcome of a game is most often based on the experience of the players rather than the luck of the draw.

It bears repeating that mah jongg is a skill-based game with an element of luck. The element of luck is out of your control. At the beginning of the game, the luck factor is 100% and so is the predictability of getting the tiles you needed because none of the tiles are visible.

Luck is offset by your experience because during the Charleston you have opportunities to transform your dealt hand. The greater the transformation, the fewer picks you will need from the wall for continued hand development which means the luck factor is diminished. After the Charleston, the luck factor is reduced with every pick and discard. As more tiles are revealed, the chances of getting the tiles you need become more predictable. When the last tile is discarded, the luck factor is zero.

---

[13] International Mind Sports Association, 2014/2002; https://imsa.sport/

During the game, players use skills like critical thinking, situational awareness, and social acuity to optimize their winning potential. The blend of knowledge, skills previously mentioned, and strategies define a playing style. The more experience a person has, the more refined their playing style becomes and the more equipped they will be to optimize their winning potential.

It takes time for players to build their knowledge, develop their skills, and learn new strategies. Someone new to the game has not had time so they must rely on luck. Someone who has played the game for years relies on informed decision-making. There is also something to be said of the dynamic of the players at the table. When people with different experience levels play together, skill prevails. When people with similar experience levels play together, luck prevails. So, while luck affects the game's outcome somewhat, a player's skill optimizes their winning potential.

Study the rules of the game to build your knowledge, develop your skills, and learn new strategies to optimize your performance regardless of how luck manifests during a game.

Attitude Check

Have you ever played mah jongg and not enjoyed it? Have you ever slammed a discard on the table? Have you ever thrown in your hand aggressively after losing? If you answered yes to any of those questions, you were "playing on tilt." Playing on tilt happens when you let disappointment or frustration dominate your mindset, potentially impairing your decision-making and taking the fun out of the game for everyone involved.

People who play games usually have a competitive streak to some degree and are in it to win it. However, losing repeatedly can feel discouraging. If you find yourself going on tilt, take a break from the game and, while you are resting, reflect.

First, think about your WHY. Do you play for social interaction? Do you play for the entertainment value? Do you play because it challenges your mind? Knowing your why will keep you grounded when things get tough.

Second, think about your attitude. Think back on recent games and try to identify how discouragement manifests itself when you lose. When you notice negative feelings while playing the game, figure out what triggers them besides the obvious, not winning.

Finally, manage your expectations! Remember that the average win rate for mah jongg players, assuming equal levels of experience and skill, is about 20% because there will be the occasional wall game. If you are expecting to win more frequently, you are putting yourself under way too much pressure.

Aptitude Check

When you find yourself in a losing streak, consider taking a break from playing. Use this opportunity to assess your skills and learn new strategies. Acknowledge your strengths and leverage them. Identify your weaknesses and look for ways to develop new skills or consider experimenting with different strategies.

Watch skill-building videos, practice at home, and then play online to test playing styles, learn new skills, and integrate strategies (Appendix B). If, after taking these steps, you still are not making progress, try working with a mentor. A mentor can observe your decision-making and help you break through your challenges.

Altitude Check

When you are ready to return to the game, prepare mentally by remembering why you like to play the game. When you're at the table, stay flexible, remain calm, be confident, and rise above challenges.

If you are hesitant to return to the tables, here are three ways to ease yourself back into the game:

> Play online: Playing with robots is an effective way to ease back into the game.

> Win little, win big: Play hands of least and slight resistance. These hands are easy to play and they are plentiful. Also, you can use lots of jokers to complete them.

> Leverage efficiency: Consider playing hands in the Consecutive Run category. This is the most powerful category on the card because there are three suits numbered 1-9 that provide flexibility and efficiency. The key is to keep four or five numbers in a range around your multiples or predominant pattern. Then gather tiles until you only have keepers. At that point, reduce your options or pick a hand. Do not limit your hands to Consecutive Run long term because you will stunt your continued growth as a player and potentially get bored of playing the same hands over and over again.

I confess that I experienced a six-week long losing streak once, and I felt so discouraged that I stopped playing for a few weeks. During that time, I studied how to handle a losing streak and created the list above to help with my mindset.

In addition to performing these four checks before playing, I set an achievable goal. Here are a few examples:

- Do not discard an opponent's winning tile
- Play a hand I have not won before
- Attempt a quint

If you are new to mah jongg, try your best to keep up with the pace of the game. If you make a mistake, you can recover or play defensively and learn by watching the other players.

Regardless of your experience, keep a clear head. Develop your critical thinking, situational awareness, and social acuity skills to improve your decision-making and gameplay. Try new strategies little by little and adopt tactics that fit your playing style. Remember to leave losses at the table and, most importantly, have fun!

There is no doubt that winning is gratifying but remember that there is much you can learn from losing. I will never have to experience another losing streak because now I consider it a learning streak.

Notes ...

Appendices

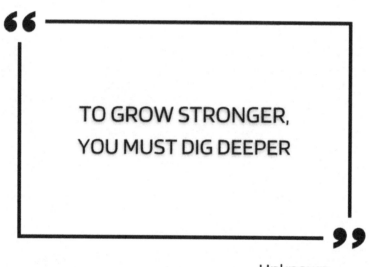

> **TO GROW STRONGER, YOU MUST DIG DEEPER**
>
> Unknown

Notes ...

Appendices

Appendix A: Mahj Life Wiki, a FREE and Searchable On-Demand Resource

On the Mahj Life website you will find a mah jongg wiki which is a free and searchable on-demand collection of mah jongg-related articles. Each article is categorized by subject matter using keyword tags. To find an article, enter either keywords or a specific article number in the search box. After reading the article, you can find tags in that page's footer that you can click to take you to an index of related articles. https://mahjlife.com/wiki

Mah jongg terms used in this book and in my YouTube, videos can be found in the wiki glossary.

If you have a situation that is not covered by a wiki article, submit ideas or content using the form found on the "Get Involved" page.

Appendix B: YouTube Videos

If you are new to American mah jongg, please visit the Mahj Life YouTube channel where you can watch American mah jongg video lessons and livestreams. If you have not already done so, subscribe and click the little grey bell to get channel notifications! https://tinyurl.com/bdfcwa38

For fundamentals and skill building exercises, look for links under the download section in the Mahj Life Wiki articles "American Mah Jongg" (article 162) and "Direct Links to NMJL YouTube Videos," including my free "New Card Analysis" eBook (article 192).

To learn even more essential skills and strategies, review the Mahj Life YouTube channel's video posting and livestream schedule. There you can find links to videos and wiki articles on various topics, to access this schedule, go to the Mahj Life wiki article "American Mah Jongg Skills and Strategies Matrix" (Article 210).

You can leave comments in the comment section below each Mahj Life YouTube video if you have any questions. You can also send me a direct email (michele@mahjlife.com).

Appendix C: Connect and Engage

Please subscribe to the Mahj Life Email list for important announcements and to receive content updates. https://mahjlife.com/email-list-subscription/

Join the following Facebook Groups to join online conversations at Michele Frizzell #MAHJLIFE, Mahjong Community, and Mah Jongg, That's It!

Find a mentor through the Mahj Life Instructor Guild directory on the Mahj Life Website.

Notes ...

Appendix D: Mock American Mah Jongg Card

The mock American mah jongg card is used in lesson videos online. To use the card outside this book cut on the dotted lines. To create a three-panel card, place them side by side (left to right), then secure them by taping the edges (front and back).

Left panel

YEAR	VALUE	
FF YYYY DDDD DDDD (Any 1 suit with any 2 Dragons)	X	25
YYYY NNNN RR SSSS (Red Dragon only)	X	25
YYYY EEEE GG WWWW (Green Dragon only)	X	25
FF YYYY DDDD NEWS (Any 2 suits)	C	30
2468		
2222 4444 6666 88 (Any 1 suit)	X	25
22 44 666 888 DDDD (Any 3 suits)	X	25
FFFF 22 44 666 888 (Any 1 suit)	X	25
FF 22 44 6666 8888 (Any 3 suits)	X	30
FF 222 44 66 888 DD (Any 2 suits)	X	30
222 44 66 888 NEWS (Any 1 suit)	C	30
LIKE NUMBERS		
FF 1111 1111 1111 (Any 3 suits, any like #s)	X	25
FF 1111 1111 NEWS (Any 2 suits, any like #s)	C	30
ADDITION		
FFFF 2222 + 8888 = 10 or FFFF 2222 + 8888 = 10	X	25
FFFF 3333 + 7777 = 10 or FFFF 3333 + 7777 = 10	X	25
FFFF 6666 + 4444 = 10 or FFFF 6666 + 4444 = 10	X	25
FFFF 9999 + 1111 = 10 or FFFF 9999 + 1111 = 10	X	25

[intentionally blank]

Middle panel

QUINTS	VALUE	
11 222 3333 44444 (Any 4 consecutive #s)	X	40
11111 11111 **DDDD** (Any 3 suits, any like numbers)	X	40
FF NNNNN DD SSSSS (Red Dragon only)	X	45
FF EEEEE DD WWWWW (Green Dragon only)	X	45

CONSECUTIVE RUN		
11 222 3333 444 55 or **55 666 7777 888 99** (Any 1 suit)	X	25
111 2222 333 4444 (Any 2 suits, any 4 con #s)	X	25
FF 111 222 333 444 (Any 2 suits, any 4 con #s)	X	25
FFFF 1111 2222 DD or **FFFF 1111 2222 DD** (Any 2 con #s)	X	25
FF 11 22 333 444 **DD** (Any 3 suits, any 4 con #s)	X	30
11 22 33 4444 5555 (Any 3 suits, any 5 con #s)	X	30
1111 22 3333 **NEWS** (Any 1 suit, any 3 con #s)	C	30

13579		
11 333 5555 777 99 (Any 1 Suit)	X	25
111 3333 333 5555 or 555 7777 777 9999 (Any 2 suits)	X	25
FF 1111 3333 5555 or **FF** 5555 7777 9999 (Any 1 suit)	X	25
111 333 555 777 99 (Any 3 suits)	X	25
FF 111 333 555 **DDD** or **FF** 555 777 999 **DDD** (Any 2 suits)	X	25
FFFF 11 33 55 **DDDD** or **FFFF** 55 77 99 **DDDD** (Any 1 suit)	X	30
1111 33 5555 **NEWS** or 5555 77 9999 **NEWS** (Any 1 suit)	C	30

[intentionally blank]

Right panel

WINDS - DRAGONS	VALUE	
NNNN EEEE WWWW SS	X	25
FF NNNN RRRR SSSS (Red Dragon only)	X	25
FF EEEE GGGG WWWW (Green Dragon only)	X	25
NNNN 11 11 11 SSSS (Any 3 suits, any like odd #s)	X	30
EEEE 22 22 22 WWWW (Any 3 suits, any like even #s)	X	30
DDDD DD DDDD NEWS (Dragons any combination)	C	30

369		
3333 6666 9999 DD (Any 1 suit)	X	25
FF 333 666 999 DDD (Any 2 suits)	X	25
FFFF 3333 66 9999 or FFFF 3333 66 9999	X	25
FF 3333 6666 9999 or FF 3333 6666 9999	X	25
33 66 99 3333 3333 (Any 3 suits, kongs can be 3, 6, or 9)	X	30
FF 333 66 999 NEWS (Any 1 suit)	C	30

SINGLES AND PAIRS		
NN EE WW SS 11 11 11 (Any like numbers)	C	50
FF 22 44 66 88 DD DD (Any 3 suits)	C	50
FF 11 33 55 77 99 DD (Any 1 suit)	C	50
11 22 33 44 55 66 77 (Any one suit, any 7 con #s)	C	50
33 66 99 33 66 99 DD (Any 3 suits)	C	50
FF YYYY YYYY NEWS (Any 2 suits)	C	75

125

[intentionally blank]

Appendix E: Risk Assessment Matrix Cutout

RISK ASSESSMENT MATRIX			Impact			
			Acceptable	Tolerable	Unacceptable	Intolerable
			Opponent has no exposures	Opponent has one exposure	Opponent has two exposures	Opponent has three exposures
Likelihood	Improbable	Risk unlikely to occur	Low	Medium	Medium	High
	Possible	Risk likely to occur	Low	Medium	High	Extreme
	Probable	Risk most likely to occur	Medium	Medium	High	Extreme

If you draw a risky tile, use good judgment.

PUSH JUDGMENT	FOLD JUDGMENT
If you think your winning tile is in the wall or that an opponent might discard it, push to win.	If you think the chances of getting your winning tile are slim, fold.
Discard the riskiest tile first so you have safer tiles to discard as the game progresses.	Keep risky tiles, break up your hand, and discard as safely as possible to force a wall game (draw).
Reassess every picked tile from the wall especially if another player makes exposures because they are pushing to win too and may have a stronger wait.	Do not claim discards for exposures because exposures give other players valuable information.

Discard jokers but save them to be your last discards because they are the only truly safe discards. |

Brought to you by Maj Life™   Questions? Send an email to care@mahjlife.com

[intentionally blank]

Appendix F: Citations

Studies on the Benefits of Playing Card Games
Dr. Jilas Paingeeri, 11/17/2022, Sprint Medical; Mental Health
Benefits of Playing Card Games, https://tinyurl.com/2fdhvts3

Gamesver Team and JC Franco, 1/7/2024, 16 Ways Playing
Card Games Can Help Your Mental Health,
https://tinyurl.com/2fdhvts3

Gamesver Team and JC Franco, 1/7/2024, 20 Powerful Benefits
and Advantages of Playing Card Games.
https://tinyurl.com/3yzyp9xv

Mind Sports
International Mind Sports Association, 2014/2002;
https://imsa.sport/

Online Platforms
I Love Mahj, https://mahjlife.com/i-love-mahj/

Mahjong Time, https://mahjlife.com/mahjong-time/

Game Theory
Adam Hayes, 3/4/2024, Game Theory,
https://tinyurl.com/3pup8fje

Travis, (date not posted), Game theory in Crazy Rich Asians,
https://tinyurl.com/yxjm929z

Dr. Linda Elder, (date not posted), Game Theory,
https://iep.utm.edu/game-th/

John von Neumann and Oskar Morgenstern, Theory of Games
and Economic Behavior, https://tinyurl.com/4cvycbw7

Sloperama
Tom Sloper, (date not posted), Strategy by Wall,
https://sloperama.com/mjfaq/mjfaq08.htm

Tom Sloper, 9/13/2009, Joker Bait,
https://www.sloperama.com/mahjongg/column423a.htm

Notes ...

Conclusion

> PURSUE EXCELLENCE WITH TENACITY.
> ACCEPT FAILURE WITH DIGNITY.
> EMBRACE SUCCESS WITH HUMILITY.

Michele Frizzell, mah jongg fanatic

Notes ...

Conclusion

Congratulations, you have made it through **American Mah Jongg Primer Volume 2, Essential Skills and Powerful Strategies You Need to Optimize Your Winning Potential**!

Well, now you know my epiphanies:

Epiphany #1 Game Theory

Epiphany #2 Profiling Players

Epiphany #3 Position and Assessing Risks

Epiphany #4 How to Harness the Power of the Charleston

Epiphany #5 Outside-In/Inside-Out Discard Strategy

I hope you found these both interesting and helpful.

Play often to develop your skills, practice new strategies to optimize your potential, and adopt what resonates with you to refine your playing style.

I wish you many years of fun and friendship playing mah jongg!

May all your picks be keepers,

Instructor, Author, Speaker

678-261-8500
michele@mahjlife.com | mahjlife.com
175 Hickory Flat Hwy, Ste. 110-335
Canton, GA 30115

MAHJ LIFE

About the Author

Michele Frizzell is an avid mah jongg player, group leader, and instructor. In 1973, she and her mom learned how to play Wright-Patterson Mah Jongg, a version popular in the military community. Michele has since learned other ways to play, including the National Mah Jongg League version. She began teaching and leading mah jongg groups in 1990. In the fall of 2017, Michele moved to rural Georgia and discovered that there were there no mah jongg players in the area. As a result, she decided to become a YouTube creator to share her lessons and skill builder drills online. As of this publication date, her YouTube channel has grown to over 33,500 subscribers, and she has published more than 2,700 videos.

Michele has two grown sons and she lives in north Georgia with her husband, David, and their poodle, Riley.

> **LEARN FAST PLAY HARD MOST IMPORTANTLY HAVE FUN!**

Michele Frizzell, mah jongg fanatic

Notes ...